WHY CUSTOMERS DO WHAT THEY DO

WHO THEY ARE, WHY THEY BUY, *and* HOW YOU CAN ANTICIPATE THEIR EVERY MOVE

MARSHAL COHEN

McGraw-Hill

New York   Chicago   San Francisco   Lisbon   London   Madrid   Mexico City
Milan   New Delhi   San Juan   Seoul   Singapore   Sydney   Toronto

1 2 3 4 5 6 7 8 9 0   DOC/DOC   0 9 8 7 6 5

ISBN 0-07-146036-5

McGraw-Hill books are available at special quantity discounts to use as premiums and sales promotions, or for use in corporate training programs. For more information, please write to the Director of Special Sales, McGraw-Hill Professional, Two Penn Plaza, New York, NY 10121-2298. Or contact your local bookstore.

 This book is printed on recycled, acid-free paper containing a minimum of 50% recycled, de-inked fiber.

*For those that helped me to explore,
educate, and elevate for this book,
I would like to express my appreciation to:
Cristina, Jeanne, Neil, Tod, Karyn, and
of course the greatest inspiration of all,
Laura and Sophie.*

Contents

Introduction

WHETHER YOU'RE A CEO, a marketing director, a brand manager, a product manager, or a consultant, I have good news for you. It doesn't matter if you're selling cars, books, information, clothes, food, electronics, or even your own services: *Why Customers Do What They Do* is going to help you get better at forecasting the variables of a changing marketplace, connect with your customer—today's consumer—to understand where that customer is going and why, and show you what you can do to develop new products and strategies that will work better than what you're doing right now. Together we will deconstruct some of the marketing myths of the past and replace them with a solid new branding and sales paradigm that focuses on what I call the Five E's: Educate, Explore, Elevate, Entertain, and Evaluate.

Drawing on the market research I've done for The NPD Group, Inc., I'm going to help you to connect with con-sumers—today's consumers, who are very different from those of a year ago or even a month ago—and show you how to keep track of the constantly moving target we call the consumer. You will get a fresh perspective on why and how their daily habits affect purchasing behavior in fundamental ways and on the way their behavior will have an impact on the marketplace and your business down the road. But you're probably still wondering about those Five E's, so let's look at them a little more closely, and then we'll really get into them later in the book.

Educate, Explore, Elevate, Entertain, and Evaluate. They're simple, and if you do them all, you will improve your marketing and sales efforts in measurable and often profound ways.

1. The first E is Educate, and it's all about communicating to everyone who needs to know about your product, your brand, or your service. Thus, it's what you have to do for the consumer, for your distributors, and for your product team internally.

2. The next E is Explore, which is what you have to do to learn who your customers are, why they buy what they buy, why they want what they want, and how you can tap into that behavior and prosper while doing it.

3. The third E is Elevate, and that is what most consumers want to do to their lifestyles and what your product probably can help them accomplish, if only they knew about it.

4. The fourth E is Entertain, and it's what helps consumers enjoy learning about your product, shopping in your store, or using your service department.

5. The final E is Evaluate, and that's what you have to do on an ongoing basis: evaluate how you're doing with those four other E's and then act on what you find.

When used together, the E's will shed light on the part of your operation that is currently in the dark and help you refine and keep refining your brand, product, or service for optimum results—and revenue.

As we go forward through the book, each chapter will look at a specific aspect of marketing and highlight the applicable E's to show how you can connect better with your customer. In Chapter 1, I'll examine what I call the "moving target" that is today's consumer and explore (that's an E) how that consumer has changed and will keep on changing, whether you like it or not. Chapter 2 explains the importance of communicating with customers in their own language and on their own terms so that they understand what your product, brand, or service is all about. Chapter 3 discusses the creation of three new brand categories and what that can mean to you and your customers. Chapter 4 takes a good hard look at the four elements of the value equation and explains how you can decide which elements of the equation you should highlight. Chapter 5 examines what I call the "thinning middle," which is the narrowing space between premium, luxury purchases and the proverbial "bargain basement" discount items. Chapter 6 sheds light on what may be the most underappreciated opportunity of all time—the constantly expanding waistline of consumers—and how underserved that market is. Chapter 7 looks at the generation gap and how that gap has narrowed and continues to narrow and even blur until a new type of market segmentation has become necessary, one categorized by lifestyle. Chapter 8 examines the Five E's in detail and in light of everything you've read to that point, Chapter 9 explores real examples of brands that are demonstrating new, pivotal directions in marketing to consumers, and Chapter 10 provides an action plan you can use to reach your customers and ultimately sell more of your product or service to them.

Along the way you'll get insights into approaches such as celebrity marketing and how it fits into the Five E's by entertaining and elevating the consumer. Today's consumer relates to celebrity marketing in a different way than ever before, a way that focuses on the lifestyle of the celebrity. People look at celebrities today for similarities in their lifestyles. They want to connect to celebrities and try to imitate them. There is an assumption made on the consumer's part that what is good for them (the celebrities) is good for us (the consumers).

Age segmentation is another area that has changed marketing and business. If you, as a manager/marketer, are trying to communicate to a 45-year-old today the way you always did in the past, it's not going to work. Today's 45-year-old dresses, exercises, and lives completely differently than he or she did a generation ago. If you are selling a product to an age group, you have to understand today's age segmentation. The young aspire to be older earlier, and the older aspire to be younger longer. Marketing to today's 45-year-old is like marketing to 35-year-olds a generation ago. Each age group has to be looked at independently, and products need to be marketed accordingly; lifestyles need to be examined or you'll never break through and sell as you want to do.

Some of the things I hope you'll understand and appreciate after reading the book are ideas such as "the thinning middle" that midlevel brands have to deal with while luxury brands become more affordable This book also will help you understand what I call the "value equation." Today managers and marketers think price is the only answer to doing better business. It's not. Value is a four-part equation that consists of price, quality, style, and service. The book will explain what I call the value equation and show how consumers think about what they buy and what affects their purchases. I'm going to help you use the value equation to understand your business better and increase your opportunities.

Why Customers Do What They Do is going to take you on a journey across several businesses to show you how to market your product or brand successfully to consumers who are increasingly immune to traditional marketing ploys. You will find examples of private branding from companies such as Wal-Mart, Target, and other department stores, and I'll explore the impact private branding has had on the entire retail scene.

Some of the industries this book will cover include technology, fashion, footwear, and video games. The iPod, for example, provides a perfect opportunity to examine why customers do what they do. Apple Computer Inc.'s approach is all about the Five E's. Apple educated and entertained the consumer in various ways about the product, elevated the consumer's awareness of the iPod, and explored new ways to deliver the product by using a website to allow the consumer to download music. Then it rolled out the Apple Store to make buying the iPod and all other Apple products easier and more satisfying.

The men's skin-care market and companies such as Estée Lauder and Lancôme are other examples of success through using the Five E's. The book will examine how those companies educated men on the benefits of skin care, elevated those products to a new comfort level, and explored new products with that demographic in mind.

Footwear is another industry in which companies are using the Five E's successfully. Merrell, the footwear company, has a very interesting story to tell. They are small but relevant. In fact, they score higher in brand relevance than any other women's footwear manufacturer does, and it's all because of how they market their brand. Merrell may not be as well known as the Nikes of the world, but they are doing so many things right that it's worth telling their story.

Why Customers Do What They Do uses hard data to support key concepts, and it will show you how to make your products and brands rise above the competition and how to stay focused and steadfast in dealing with your strategic goals. These easy-to-use marketing methods are based on years of experience working with manufacturers, brand managers, and consumers across the country. Hard numbers from The NPD Group's point-of-sale (POS) tracking service, which includes data from hundreds of retail companies, and NPD's consumer panel of more than 2 million people will give you insights and information not found anywhere else, and when you're done reading, you're truly going to understand why customers do what they do.

1

CONNECTING WITH A MOVING TARGET

I HAVE SEEN MORE CHANGES in consumer purchasing behavior in the last two years than I have in the last two decades. Why? Because consumers today are part of a world that is moving at lightning-fast speed. They are seeing new products and enhanced features introduced at a mind-boggling rate, and the lifestyles of individuals have become increasingly multidimensional and multifaceted. With so many added choices in the marketplace and new needs to fill, customers have more purchasing decisions to make, and those decisions are far more complex than ever before.

Take buying something as simple as toothpaste, for example. Two decades ago there were about three major brands and about five or so varieties of toothpaste from which a consumer could choose. A pretty easy purchasing decision, right? Today there are 77 (and this number

Lifestyle Marketing

Consumers today are more interested in brands from companies that understand their complex lifestyles. It is not enough to market your brand to a specifically targeted consumer. The interests and needs of consumers, along with their distractions, have grown at huge rates, and your brand must measure up to all these elements to succeed.

is growing) different varieties of toothpaste in the marketplace. Thus, a consumer has a much bigger decision to make: What are all the different choices, and which benefits do I really want? Do I want the one that provides fluoride/cavity protection, tartar control, fresh breath, tooth whiteners, or some combination of these? What flavor do I want, and what flavor do my kids and others in the house prefer? Do I want a gel or a paste, a tube that can stand up or one that lies flat?

You get the idea. It's a much more involved purchasing decision, and it's only one of many with which today's consumers must grapple. And don't get me started on the number of different toothbrushes available now.

In a marketplace that continues to change at warp speed and offers an ever-increasing array of new and innovative products for consumers to purchase with their limited dollars, companies today can't afford to use yesterday's marketing formulas. As competition for the customer's wallet intensifies, it is critical for companies to understand the drivers of change and respond to the related effects of those factors on consumer buying behavior. Trends that affect that behavior start with technological advances in all fields of product development. These advances are creating new customer needs and wants, making decisions more complicated, giving consumers a greater ability to research products in advance, and fueling the emergence of a disposable product society. Developments in retailing and branding strategies are changing where consumers shop, what they spend their money on, and the trade-offs they make between service and price.

TRENDS THAT ARE CHANGING HOW WE BUY

Without a doubt, advances in technology have had the most profound and far-reaching impact on innovations and new product introductions in the consumer marketplace. With its "unlimited brain power," the computer is helping to design products and product features that only recently were not even imagined by the human mind. Thanks to advancing technology from as far afield as electronics and food science, companies now deliver products that are bigger (or smaller), better, faster, and

Enhanced Products

More and more businesses across industries are introducing technological advances into their products. Eighteen percent of the apparel being produced today features hassle-free fabric, and wrinkle-free pants are just the beginning. Today you can buy beauty products with sunscreen, light-sensitive eyewear, and fat-busting food products. These product enhancements have been a deciding factor for consumers.

cheaper, and they introduce them into the market more quickly than ever before. Think about what we consume today. Everyday products such as DVDs, MP3s, Blackberrys, and cellular camera phones and features such as digital, high-definition, plasma, flat screen, and wide screen are examples of things that didn't exist a few short years ago, and the pace is *not* slowing. Quite the contrary.

A sea change is taking place in product design as technology is being applied to the quest for state-of-the-art living. These advances are creating unprecedented decision-making issues for the consumer (see Fig. 1-1). Let's examine some of the issues consumers face in making these decisions.

FIGURE 1-1   Have you ever used apparel products with these features? The graph shows the percentage of consumers who have used apparel with these characteristics. It's interesting to note that for pants with an expandable waist, the number for 45-year-olds levels out at 39% and jumps to 55% for those age 55 and older.

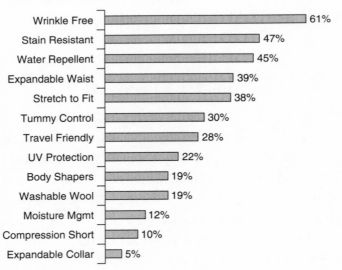

SOURCE: The NPD Enhanced Product Study.

I DIDN'T EVEN KNOW I WANTED THAT

Product enhancements are designed to make consumers' lives easier, better, more convenient, and more enjoyable. More important, new and expanded product offerings are *creating* new needs and wants. Not long ago people were satisfied to use daytimers and calendars to keep track of their schedules. Now millions of people can't live without their Palm Pilots. For some consumers it's not good enough to use an old-fashioned ice cream scoop anymore: They want today's latest ergonomic model that will get a scoop out with less hand stress, making for a more enjoyable ice cream experience. In the process of designing your product or even your brand strategy, the vision of where either one will be over the course of the next several years and where product enhancements can take your business over the long term must be explored.

IT'S HARD TO MAKE UP MY MIND

More offerings mean not only making more decisions but making more complicated decisions. With so many new products and varieties available, today's decision isn't simply a matter of whether to put milk and sugar in our coffee. Rather, it's what flavor coffee we want and whether we want a latté or mocha, decaf or regular, tall or grandé. In the past people who needed to correct their vision made a choice among the eyeglass frames or contact lenses they would wear. Now, thanks to advances in technology and medicine, their choices have been expanded to include the possibility of laser eye surgery, making for a much more complex decision.

I NEED TO DO MY HOMEWORK

Dealing with more offerings and often an overwhelming number of choices requires better information and education.

Many products or features simply didn't exist not long ago, and so a consumer today must learn about many new things. First, what products are currently available to fill a particular need? What are the differences among them, along with the advantages and disadvantages of each one? And where can I find information to help with the decision making?

Think about your own purchasing behavior and how you make your buying decisions. No doubt that process has changed over time. Have you shopped for a new computer lately? It takes research and knowledge to make an informed and appropriate decision about which features to choose: how much memory you'll need and whether you need a CD or DVD burner or a wireless Internet card. The list goes on.

Not only do today's consumers have to learn about purchasing products and services, they also need to be certain that they are spending their money wisely. Consider home mortgages. Most home buyers used to get a 30-year fixed-rate mortgage from the local bank and hold it until it was paid off. Today they can get a mortgage from hundreds of lenders that offer 10-, 15-, and 30-year maturities with fixed or adjustable rates, amortizing or "interest only" payments, collateralized or no money down. It's no small feat to make sense of it all. Consumers need to spend time and effort getting the information they need to make an intelligent decision.

Fig. 1-2 shows some of the many sets of knowledge consumers are expected to have today.

Consumers need to be jacks- and jills-of-all-trades. They must be versed in diet and nutrition, financially savvy, and in the know about how to travel safely and pack efficiently. They must know where to shop for the best bargains or indulge in luxury items, be proficient in using the Internet and digital cameras, and be knowledgeable about

FIGURE 1-2   A consumer today must be all of the following.

- Dietitian
- Tech Guru
- Chauffeur
- Efficiency Expert
- Fashion Coordinator
- Pharmacist
- Psychologist
- Investment Counselor
- Party Planner
- Nutritionist

- Travel Agent
- Teacher's Aide
- Handyman
- Chef
- Veterinarian
- Car Mechanic/Enthusiast
- Athletic Trainer
- Entertainment Director
- Bargain Hunter
- Mom or Dad

SOURCE: NPD Fashionworld.

purchasing a computer and banking online. It is necessary to be skilled in entertaining our kids, dogs, and spouses and to know how to be a better parent. Customers who like to shop at The Home Depot or Lowe's must even be competent in plumbing, home repairs, and landscape design.

Just where do consumers get information and learn all these skills? We learn much of it from "snippets": from articles in magazines and newspapers and from three-minute segments on television that feature so-called experts telling consumers how to do this and that. The other sources include water cooler conversations and the Internet.

NEXT YEAR'S MODEL WILL BE EVEN BETTER

We live in a "disposable product" society today. The quest for quality and longevity has been replaced by the desire to stay current. Buyers don't mind replacing their purchases frequently, as that enables them to keep up with the product improvements that undoubtedly will be made.

In fact, many consumers tell me that they would rather buy a new blender for $14.99, knowing it may break in a year or two, than spend $89.99 for a significantly higher-quality one that will last much longer. They prefer to buy the less expensive one, figuring that even if they have to buy four or five blenders in the next 10 or so years, they will be ahead of the game financially *and* keep up with the latest in blender technology.

Even big-ticket items are disposable today. More and more people are leasing cars. This way they can get a new car every two or three years and take advantage of new safety features and design enhancements.

HOW SHOULD I SPEND MY MONEY?

Consumers have a limited amount of income to spend on discretionary purchases. Having more choices means allocating the same number of dollars across a broader range of goods and services, and so we have seen shifts in consumer spending as clients migrate money to new and different products and services. As you can see in Fig. 1-3, American consumers, both young and old, have shifted their spending priorities to gadgets, shoes, beauty and health care, and eating out. The figure shows the diverse spending and the purchase power each category offers. But

FIGURE 1-3 Let's do the math. Here's how income is spent by the average consumer in the United States.

- Average Income in the United States is   45k
- After taxes   <u>41k</u>
- Housing   13k
- Transportation   8k
- Food   5k
- Insurance/Pension   4k
- Apparel/Services   3k
- Health Care   2k
- Entertainment   <u>2k</u>
- Left for Discretionary Spending   4k
  - $333/month
    - Telecommunications (TV/Phone/Cell) $173/mo ⎤
    - Gym $ 24/mo ⎦ (2/3 spent)

SOURCE: **US Department of Labor Statistics.**

with finite dollars, something had to give, and apparel is one of the categories that are losing wallet share.

Economic conditions also have been playing an increasingly large role in how freely consumers spend their money on discretionary purchases. In recent years the media have bombarded people with daily updates on jobless claims, financial markets, gas price increases, the war in Iraq, recession predictions, and expert opinions on how the economy is faring. In the wake of the uncertainty this information has created, we have seen buyers stick to necessities and tighten their purse strings by putting off discretionary purchases. In fact, more than half of all consumers have reported that rising fuel costs are affecting their spending.

More recently, with signs of the economy rebounding, we are beginning to see more spending and more impulse purchases. Of course, the economy has always had its ups and downs, but consumers are reacting to the economic environment more rapidly because the information is so readily available.

I'LL STOP AT TARGET AFTER I GO TO MY FAVORITE UPSCALE DEPARTMENT STORE

Where do consumers go to get the products they are learning about daily? They are shopping in discount stores *along with* department and specialty stores. In fact, one of every two consumers who shops in a department store also shops in a discount store. Consumers are less loyal to any single channel type of retailer than they were in the past.

Shoppers today are buying basics at big-box retailers such as Costco, Target, and Wal-Mart, seeking commodities at everyday low prices or specials at holiday times with prices that can't be beat. Finding bargains makes shopping fun, and this has been drawing men back into stores.

Although for many consumers *price* remains the driving factor in purchase decisions, *service* has captured the top spot in the minds of others. For these shoppers it is not just about price anymore. After all, what good is a newfangled gadget if you have no clue about how to assemble it or use it or even know if it is working properly? Thus, customer support from the retailer becomes highly valued, even if it means paying extra. We'll discuss this more in Chapter 5.

SHOPPING TODAY—AND TOMORROW

What does the future hold for how and where consumers will shop? With more and more people becoming more comfortable with *shopping* as well as *learning* online, the Internet is going head-to-head with traditional retailers. Although today's younger generation has grown up with computers, consumers who are not Internet-savvy are relying on those who are to assist them. Grandparents are depending on their grandchildren to help them learn more about the world of technology, and they're using the Internet in increasing numbers.

We are seeing a return to *relationship retailing,* in which consumers can feel comfortable purchasing something out of their comfort zone, knowing they have a place to call for help—a place where they will be welcomed when they seek answers no matter how often the question is asked or how basic the question may be. Visit an Apple Store and you can speak with a "Genius" or visit a Best Buy and seek out its "Geek Squad" and you'll see what I mean firsthand. We are seeing the future now, and in many ways it resembles the past. Consumers want good, old-fashioned personal service and will shop in venues where it is provided.

Relationship retailing helps the consumer feel comfortable, connected, and committed to the retailer.

Consumers who rely on this type of interaction are willing to pay more for the experience. The return of Main Street, mom-and-pop retailers is about to emerge with major chains such as Wal-Mart opening Wal-Mart Village stores. The major discounters are establishing relationship retailing environments by opening smaller stores with more personalized elements. The hardware franchise TrueValue is another example of this trend in which small local stores take advantage of national advertising while delivering a personal relationship element to their customers. Franchising may well be the future for small local merchants.

Relationship retailing offers what people want: product, knowledge, and service. Where would you rather shop for your next home computer system: at a store that will sell it to you at the lowest price but where they can't tell you how to set it up because the salesperson was working in the lamp department during his or her first two weeks of training or at a shop where the owner can help you choose what's right for you and then set it up and teach you how to use it and will even be there to answer your questions when you somehow forget what you are supposed to do with that blue cord that looks like it could fit into the phone jack?

With so many products and varieties crowding the marketplace, it is absolutely essential that the brand itself establish a connected relationship with the consumer. To succeed, it's not going to be as simple as selling commodities on the basis of price and higher-end products on the basis of relationships. It will be about getting connected

> Your brand and product must be marketed in a way
> that connects with the consumers—that tells them
> that you understand what's important to them and
> helps them choose your offerings from among a host of
> competitors in the same space.

with the consumer (more on this in the next chapter) and about which brands have relevance to the consumer's lifestyle. The brands that do the best job of associating and relating the features and benefits of their products with their target consumers' needs and wants will be the winners in the brand wars.

At the same time that advancing technology has been causing changes in consumer behavior, we also have seen changes occurring as a result of other outside influences.

OUR WORLD AND OUR WALLET

Our attitudes and outlook on the world around us affect the way we behave. Major events affect the way consumers feel. Think about the impact horrific events such as 9/11, the tsunami of 2004, and hurricane Katrina had on all of us. The terrorist attacks on September 11, 2001, were a dramatic point in many people's lives, one that rocked their sense of security and clearly changed consumer behavior. Just think what happens today when a group of emergency vehicles pass by with sirens screaming, indicating that some sort of mishap or disaster has occurred. Although everyday occurrences don't necessarily take us back to 9/11, our behavior has changed because of it. People may think very differently about travel and taking a vacation. Where to go, how to get there (drive versus fly), the state of affairs for American tourists since the war in Iraq, whether to go away at all—these are new concerns that are weighing on our minds as we seek to travel.

Before those events consumers had started to demonstrate their desire to spend more time and money on their homes and were investing in home improvement items that were practical and long-lasting rather than indulgent. Practical outweighed impressive. New automobiles were all about function over glitz, and SUV sales soared.

World events exacerbated that trend and, combined with the lowering of interest rates, resulted in a real estate boom and the emergence of the home design market. We saw a proliferation of renovation and upgrading among home owners, and those who had never owned a home before rushed to buy the first one. Nationwide, almost all consumers began purchasing items that made their homes or apartments more secure, cozier, and more comfortable places. They also invested in personal and home electronics, and so now they had a safe dwelling where they could keep up to date on all the news events or shut out the outside world completely. Consumers focused on getting faster Internet connections and more television stations with enhanced viewing via cable or satellite and on a bigger and better television. Personal electronics such as cell phones became a critical purchase.

World and national events reinforced the need and desire to focus on family and community, and purchasing behavior reflected that shift. Clothing sales, which took a huge hit after September 11, 2001, showed signs of growth only in the kids' market. The next year was a little better, but it seemed that when parents were spending on kids, they were not spending on themselves. There was a clear trade-off: When spending on kids went up, spending on adults went down. It has remained that way ever since. Electronics started to rebound in a big way in 2002. Cell phones became a must-have item, and the cellular industry established the family plan, demonstrating its understanding of the shift toward family and creating an entirely new way to keep its customers connected and in turn connect with them.

TWO CENTS FROM THE LITTLE ONES

Today's successful marketers don't overlook the increasing influence that kids have on household purchasing. This is not only a matter of which cereal or cookies to buy. Today's tech-savvy kids weigh in on decisions about expensive items such as computers, TV systems, DVD and CD players, and even which car and car entertainment system to get—and their parents are listening. What's more, with more disposable income in kids' wallets than ever before, kids and teens are consumers of high-end gadgets such as iPods, cell phones, laptops, and more.

THE CHANGING WOMAN CONSUMER

The phenomenon of women entering and leaving the workforce has changed consumer behavior significantly in recent years. Data from the U.S. Bureau of Labor and Statistics show that the increases of the 1990s in the number of working women have been shifting to declines in recent years. The number of women age 25 to 54 who are not in the workforce increased 13 percent from 1999 to 2003, a decline of 8.8 million women (see Fig. 1-4).

Today we see more and more women either working from home in a more entrepreneurial way or not working at all. Some women are discovering that it is better financially and otherwise for the household to do without the second income and the extra expenses for child care, wardrobe, and other career costs.

So what are the effects of having fewer women in the workplace? This trend has changed the dynamics of spending across several industries, from the clothing a woman purchases to her frequency of eating out. It has changed the consumption patterns of domestic goods

Societal Influencers

- World and National Events
    - 9/11
    - Military operations in Iraq, Afghanistan, and around the world
    - Columbine shooting
    - Tsunami of 2004
    - Spending by kids and teens
    - More and more discretionary funds
    - Purchasing decisions about household electronics, personal electronics, autos, and other household items
    - Hurricane Katrina
- Women
    - Decreased number of women in the corporate world

FIGURE 1-4a Women in the workforce are shifting consumer dynamics. The following graph of female monthly labor force participation rates includes females who are employed and those who are seeking employment. The period covered is September 1998 through December 2001.

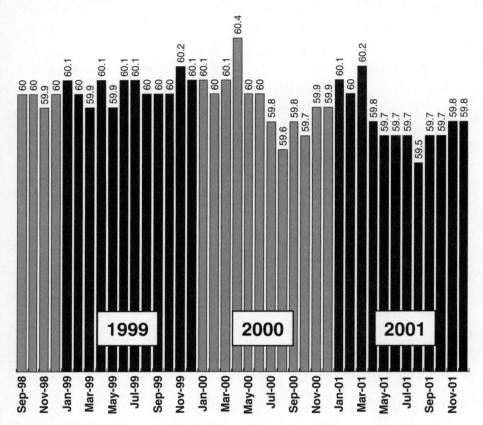

SOURCE: U.S. Bureau of Labor Statistics.

FIGURE 1-4b   This graph is a continuation of Figure 1.4a, covering the period of January 2002 through July 2004.

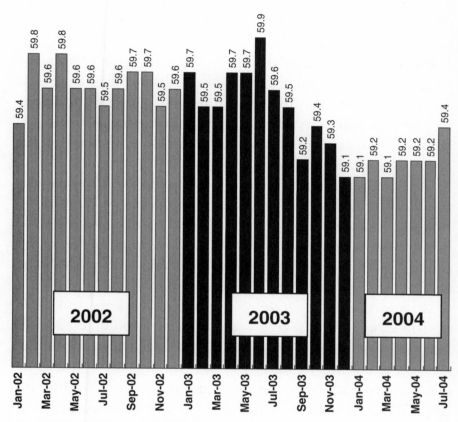

SOURCE: U.S. Bureau of Labor Statistics.

such as sheets and towels and even appliances. How so? If a woman is not working, she is more likely to be aware of the lack of effectiveness of the household clothes dryer. She also is more likely to be aware of the state of the sheets and towels if she is doing the laundry. Even the slightest shift in the pattern of women staying home and doing more domestic chores will result in a change in spending habits. Some might argue that without the extra income, certain purchases may be put off, but the numbers tell us that consumers actually are eating out more in recent years, appliance sales are healthy, and spending on home furnishings continues to grow.

All told, this slight decline in the number of women in the workforce has had a dramatic impact for marketers. Imagine finding almost 2 million new consumers who have a different take on your product. Now imagine ignoring those 2 million consumers by not addressing their needs or not recognizing their new values, wants, and lifestyles.

In addition to lifestyle changes, the *thinking* and *decision-making processes* of women have changed. Much like the women before them, they are complex, but they are more complex today because we live in a world of contradictions. Decisions are not simply black and white for a modern woman with many contradictory lifestyle issues. She is more educated yet thirsts for more knowledge. She attempts to be frugal and thrifty but likes to indulge. She is more adventurous but is cautious. The 9/11 travel issue is a great example of how these contradictions play into decision making. Women still tend to want to travel to exotic places but think twice before doing it and in many cases will not pursue a trip because of the danger or timing. They gather information and then assess the risk versus the reward and base their decision on that (see Fig. 1-5).

FIGURE 1-5 How would you define your customer?

The Modern Woman
- Age of Contradictions
  - Adventurous yet Cautious
  - Practical yet Indulgent
  - Confident yet Seeking Acceptance
  - Mature yet Youthful
  - Single yet Maternal
  - Educated yet Thirsty for Knowledge
  - Feminine yet Corporate
  - Career-Oriented yet Domesticated
- Market Accordingly   Think Lifestyle

SOURCE: *Beyond the Data with Marshal Cohen.*

REACHING TODAY'S CONSUMER

Keep in mind how today's consumer is very different from the consumer of a few years ago as we journey through the following chapters. Modern consumers are

- Looking for better, cheaper, faster, longer-lasting, and disposable products all at the same time.

- Interested in brands that others will endorse but that their contemporaries don't have yet.

- Researching where and when to make particular purchases.

- Expecting retailers to educate them on their purchases but at the same time are willing to shop in places that don't have customer service in order to pay less.

- Looking for bargains and uniqueness: investment items that will last a lifetime and some that will be thrown away, to be replaced in a year or so.

Consumers have become more complex, more educated, more demanding, and more willing to think twice or even

Consumers today are shopping in more types of stores than they did in the past. It used to be that shoppers at a certain income level shopped only in a certain type of store. Income produces no barriers today, and the same consumer will shop in the highest-price stores as well as the lowest-price ones (see Fig. 1-6).

FIGURE 1-6   Overall shopping for the preceding 12 months by store type. The percentages indicate the proportion of consumers who shopped in each type of store.

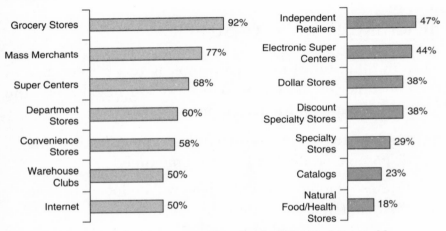

Grocery Stores	92%	Independent Retailers	47%
Mass Merchants	77%	Electronic Super Centers	44%
Super Centers	68%	Dollar Stores	38%
Department Stores	60%	Discount Specialty Stores	38%
Convenience Stores	58%	Specialty Stores	29%
Warehouse Clubs	50%	Catalogs	23%
Internet	50%	Natural Food/Health Stores	18%

SOURCE: The NPD Consumer Spending Study, NPD Fashionworld.

three times before making a purchase. The challenge for you is to learn how not only to survive in this environment but to thrive, and the Five E's will guide you through this effort.

THE THREE FACES OF THE CONSUMER

The consumer of the moment falls into one of three categories: committed, conscious, and diversified. The first group of consumers has made a firm commitment to spending their extra income on lifestyle-enhancing products and services. From cable TV to bottled water, committed consumers make purchasing decisions that will improve their lifestyles, eating away at whatever money is left in their wallets to buy other discretionary products. Learning about this trade-off will help you build a more refined brand strategy that can compete for discretionary income. Fig. 1-7 shows how committed consumers spend their money.

The conscious consumer reacts to causes and philanthropic gestures made by brands. From Paul Newman's popcorn, spaghetti sauce, and salad dressings to Nike's Live-Strong silicone bracelet, a portion of whose sales revenue is donated to specific charities, consumers are responding to social causes and contributing through their purchases.

Diversified consumers spend across a wide range of products that address the broadest spectrum of their

FIGURE 1-7   **How committed are consumers? The graph indicates the percentage of consumers using each of the categories listed.**

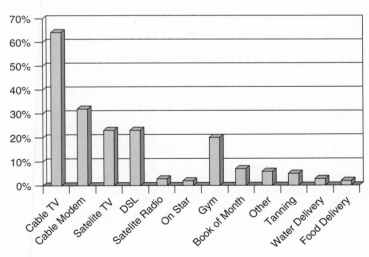

SOURCE: NPD Group.

needs. Bigger, stronger, smaller, faster, concentrated, and even organic—all are qualities that diversified consumers believe will help them better their lives.

Now that we've discussed the profile of the modern consumer, the next chapter examines how your brand can better reach this moving target.

2

DO YOU BOGO?

DO YOU KNOW WHAT BOGO IS? I was watching a woman look at a sign from outside a store. She had her head tipped to the side and obviously was confused. I asked her what she thought the sign meant. She chuckled and said she was trying to figure that out. Thinking out loud, she said that she understood that the store was having a sale but didn't see what Bogo the Clown had to do with it. She wondered if she should come back with her kids to get some footwear on sale and see the clown at the same time.

I laughed, knowing that BOGO is an industry term describing the format of a type of sale. But how was the consumer to know that BOGO means "Buy One, Get One"? And why would any retailer try to reach customers in a language so far removed from their own?

The woman left, never going into the store to see Bogo the Clown. This was not an isolated incident. In my practice I spend quite a bit of time in the field, watching shoppers, and I made sure to follow up on this as I traveled across the country two days later. While in a mall on the West Coast, I watched as a man pondered the words at the same kind of store. He looked like a confused puppy, and so of course I asked him what the sign meant. Very much like the woman, he recognized that they were having a sale, but he thought that BOGO was some kind of brand of shoes. Not interested in the BOGO brand, he didn't realize what the retailer was offering and headed off to a competitor to see if it had the shoes he wanted at a discount.

Both encounters underscore the importance of establishing clear, meaningful communications with your customers. Understand them, speak to them in their own language, find out what drives them to buy what they buy, and adopt the language, techniques, and means needed to reach them. In short, Educate, Explore, and Entertain.

BRING THE LEARNING HOME

Understanding who your customers are—not just what they buy but the types of lives they lead, where they live and how, and their habits and long-term aspirations—is what will inform your message. Learning this takes hard work. At NPD we invest a great deal of time surveying consumers, observing shoppers in the field, and dissecting the thinking that lies behind brand strategies. These are worthwhile efforts that will enable your team to craft a message and select a medium that will touch an emotional chord in your customers. Forget about the *voice* of the customer: Look at how he or she *responds* to your message. And then test that thinking. Have outsiders—people who would be your everyday consumers, ones who have no idea of what you do, what you are trying to sell, or what the product or service offers—tell you what they see in the pieces of your product and your message. Don't presell them; don't even let them know why you're asking for their opinion. Just ask them to comment on what you present. Stand back, listen, and don't respond. Absorb it. Take it away and address it as you see fit later. We all know that we get only one chance to make a first impression, and that is also true in the marketing relationship. Once you introduce additional information, you have jaded the response and it will not reflect that of an actual consumer.

Seek out and learn to read the responses of everyday people and go back to others later on, after you have made your adjustments. Don't assume that they know what you mean. Make sure they do because brands are complex organisms that in many cases have the dual responsibility of representing the core attributes of the entire organization and communicating the benefits of the company and its products to the broadest possible audience—sometimes all in a 30-second spot.

We buy and sell products and services in an increasingly complex world that requires marketers to craft a direct message to their customers. Crafting and disseminating that message so that it meets the strategic requirements of your brand is not an easy task. It requires doing a great deal of research—sometimes homegrown, sometimes commissioned—and educating the product teams.

It's no longer about the *voice* of the customer. Observe how he or she *responds* to your message and then test that thinking.

That brings me to one of my top commandments: Never, ever rely on someone else to spread your message for you. You must take your finely honed brand image directly to the consumer.

Do you remember a few years back when Firestone tires on the Ford Explorer SUV were shredding while the vehicle was in motion? The news made headlines all over the nation, and the ramifications for Bridgestone/Firestone Inc. were enormous, as the faulty product threatened to destroy the reputation of the entire company. The fact that the tires were on vehicles sold by Ford presented Firestone with the chance to let Ford to be the messenger since it was Ford customers who were directly affected. However, Firestone chose a different route, opting for a broadcast and print advertising campaign that communicated openly, honestly, and, most important, directly with the consumer about the situation. It also replaced up to 13 million of the tires, making this the largest tire recall in U.S. history. In the ads, which centered on the theme "Making It Right," Bridgestone/Firestone President, Chairman, and CEO John Lampe explained the company's position and stood proudly, reassuring consumers that Firestone was taking full responsibility. That approach allowed Firestone to get out in front of a public relations nightmare, convincing the public that it had taken the proper next steps so that they should remain committed to the brand, and preserved the company's stature in the investment community.

Firestone's strategy was based on a deep understanding of its customers' concerns, wants, and needs. It amazes me how many companies miss the opportunity to reach their customers because they simply don't listen. Again, craft your message and test it in the field. Don't wait until a catastrophic product event occurs. Start now.

Take your finely honed brand image directly to the
consumer. Never rely on someone else to spread
your message for you.

Connecting with the consumers, understanding how and
what they think about your product, must inform all of
your product and branding efforts. Another command-
ment: It's what the consumer thinks that matters.

WHY THEY BUY WHAT THEY BUY

Exploring the underlying forces behind consumer choices
is the key to maintaining your competitive edge. Your product or service may have varied features yin and yang, but if
it comes in only one color, you probably have lost your market. Really. Our research has shown that the number one
purchase influencer is style, which includes color, followed
closely by price, comfort, and fit. Although this makes perfect sense for apparel (see Fig. 2-1), it's an exciting new
trend in household and kitchen appliances, cell phones,
iPods, and other personal and home electronics. It's easy
enough to manufacture a computer in shiny apple-red, but
you need to make sure to create a clear message to consumers, announcing that your products come in a broad
array of fabulous colors.

Will the consumer buy a new washer and dryer just
because they now come in blue? Not really, but when the
time comes and they need to replace those items, they
may choose the Kenmore brand because it is offered in
their favorite color. The process is symbiotic: Tapping into

The only thing that matters is what the *customer* thinks.

FIGURE 2-1   What factors influence apparel purchasing? The numbers indicate percentages of consumers affected by each factor. The four highest percentages are circled.

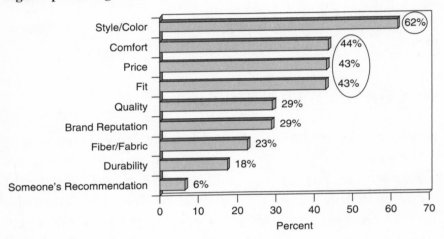

SOURCE: NPD Fashionworld.

a primary influencer such as color allows you to reach the consumer at an emotional level and create a relationship that is seen as personal. Consumers feel that your brand truly understands their needs and desires, and they believe that if your brand does that, you probably make products that understand all their needs better. Now you've got a customer for life. When you explore and identify the trends that influence purchasing, you have learned powerful information that should be used to shape your products, marketing strategies, and long-term relationship with your market.

GETTING TO KNOW YOU

It's easy to say that you *know* your customers and the trends that influence what they buy, but you also must ask yourself, "Who is my customer?" Ask your team. Go ahead. Typically, the answer you'll get is based on a demographic: middle to upper income, drives a minivan, reads one or two books a year, likes movies, works as a manager, has 2.3 kids, and is 37.5 years old. Nice profile, right? As a profile it works, but how does a profile truly help you get inside the head of your customer—get at the inner person? It's only when you get to know the psyche of your customers that you'll be able to apply the Five E's. Be forewarned: It's not pretty in there!

Consumers today are much more complex than ever before. First, purchases often range across a very wide range of products so that the lifestyle of choice (adventure-loving family of four, for instance) can be achieved. Second, there are the dynamics that individuals today must endure at every level, whether national, personal, or workplace-related. We live in a world of contradictions, and professionals need to incorporate that point in their product messages. If your brand can communicate this understanding, it will prove to consumers that your brand and your company relate to their complex lifestyle. Consumers are looking to surround themselves with brands, people, and products that understand the intricate world in which they live.

NPD Fashionworld consumer segments include the following:

- No Frills shoppers
- Grab and Go shoppers
- Sporty Value shoppers

- Classic Sophisticate shoppers
- Copycat shoppers
- Fashion for Less shoppers
- Fashion Socialite shoppers

For instance, across apparel shoppers, NPD Fashion-world identified seven types of customers (see Fig. 2-2):

1. *No Frills shoppers* are focused on "just the basics." More concerned with comfort and price than with fashion or style, they shop primarily at discount stores and buy apparel on the basis of price, not brand.

2. *Grab and Go shoppers* are physically active, mostly male shoppers who are not concerned with how they dress. They dislike shopping for clothes, and so they "replacement shop." They do not have a clear channel preference but shop at discount stores, sport specialty stores, and national chains.

FIGURE 2-2   The level of fashion involvement by market segment. Percentage of buyers within each segment among those classified (January–March 2003).

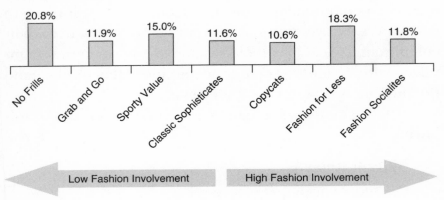

SOURCE: NPD Fashionworld.

Consumers and the lives they lead are increasingly complex.

3.   *Sporty Value shoppers* are physically active, heavily committing their time to outdoor activities such as camping, team sports, yard work, and gardening.

4.   *Classic Sophisticate shoppers* are female customers with higher household incomes. They shop for apparel on the basis of quality and style, not price, and are more likely to shop at department and upscale specialty stores for apparel and buy classic-styled brands than are the other segments.

5.   *Copycats* are less secure shoppers who look for specific brands when shopping. They are more likely to buy a particular brand that they perceive as helping them "fit in." Copycats will spend more for popular brands; fashion is important to them, but they are more likely to be trend followers than fashionistas.

6.   *Fashion for Less shoppers* are individuals who like to shop and try on the latest fashions but don't like to spend a lot of money on high-fashion apparel. Price is more important than brand name to them, but they dress to look their best at all times.

7.   *Fashion Socialites* are young, hip students and professionals who consider fashion and style a priority. They enjoy being with people with great style and taste, are not necessarily concerned with price, and shop at department and specialty stores. Fashion Socialites are highly active in many sports and social activities.

ENTERTAINMENT VALUE

Automobiles are a great place to look at ways to take your message to the next level and not only connect with consumers but keep them wanting more. I observed a number of families shopping for new cars at a local dealership. When it came time to choose the color and the model, you'd be surprised at who in the family wielded the clout: More and more, kids are involved in the decision-making process.

General Motors recognized this and began offering a minivan with a Warner Brothers package that includes a DVD player and other entertainment features to keep small passengers happy. And happy passengers make for happy drivers. In its advertising, GM incorporates the entertainment value of its products into its product message.

Related to this is work I did with Chrysler before I joined NPD. This work involved a brand extension product for its Jeep division. We made apparel and accessories that carried the Jeep lifestyle and sold it to retailers and at special events. What I learned while working with Chrysler was that when the company analyzed the sales of its minivans, it began to realize that women were driving the vehicles more than men were. Seeing this, Chrysler redesigned its minivans to be more family-friendly and less commercial and industrial. How did they do that? By bringing women onto the design teams. That was their secret

Consumers today see value in being entertained. Convenience, ease of use, and multifaceted features equal entertainment value.

weapon: Chrysler was going to revolutionize the minivan market by having women design the product. The key to this effort were added features such as ease of third-row seating setup and breakdown, sliding door positioning, and multiside doors. Entertainment value includes convenience, ease of use, and meeting all types of lifestyle requirements.

BUT WHAT DO YOU DO WHEN . . .

You've educated your product teams, delved into the psyche of your customer, and created products with features that will keep customers coming back to you for new offerings. But now you want to grow your market base, and doing that means leveraging all types of retail environments, including self-service. This is a challenging task when your primary goal is to make your brand stick in the minds of consumers. The vastness of stores such as Wal-Mart, Target, Home Depot, and Kmart works against the visibility of your product message, and without that message to guide them, consumers are truly flying solo.

While in a Home Depot branch, I observed a female shopper in her mid-forties shopping for a kitchen faucet. She played with a few floor samples, turning the handles and moving the faucets as if she expected water to flow out of the displays. She did that for almost four minutes. She played with this one and that one but kept coming back to one particular model. She looked at the price, noted that the inventory was on shelf section F, and found the product quickly enough. Clutching the faucet to her chest, she walked proudly to the checkout counter, making use of a self-checkout kiosk, and proceeded to pay for the item.

All in all the whole experience took her 12 minutes. Excellent, right? Not so. Although the process took only 12 minutes and was a relatively pain-free experience for the woman, there was one problem, which I explained to her when I approached her in the parking lot. After I introduced myself and explained what I do, and reassured her that I was *not* a stalker, I asked if she was aware of the special wrench she was going to need to undo the nut on the old faucet. She looked at me, perplexed. I explained that she would need to remove the old faucet to put in the new one and that she would be lucky if the wrench from her new purchase was the right fit for the old faucet. I also asked if she knew the size of the water connection fittings, if they were half-inch or three-quarter-inch fittings. She had no idea. I explained why this was important. I then asked her what type of sink she had and if it was a top mount or under-the-counter mount. She wasn't quite sure, but after a brief discussion it sounded more like a top mount. I explained that she needed putty to reapply to the underside of the top mount that would sit on the countertop to prevent water from getting under the sink and dripping into the cabinet. She had no idea what I was trying to explain. At that point I suggested that she go back into the store and find a sales associate to assist her in learning how to improve her kitchen faucet. To this day I get e-mails from her thanking me for saving her marriage. She explained that if she had tried to change the faucet and her husband had learned that she had bought

Self-service is a trade-off between convenience and the benefits of relationship selling.

the wrong items, was missing tools, or had a leak under the sink, she never would have been able to live it down.

Although self-service is great to some degree, we lose all contact with the consumer. What if this woman brought the faucet home without the benefit of my instructions? She would have had to make several trips back to the store and no doubt would have grown quite frustrated with the process, so much so that it might have persuaded her to stop shopping there. The bigger question is: What did the store learn from her initial purchase decision? Only the style or model that she chose. In this situation there is no communication with the consumers to learn what they want but might not find. How does this help you design products and create promotions that speak to your core audience?

This is not a healthy way to maximize one's business. In this case there was no one to add on to the sale either. Although self-service is something consumers state they want because they want to check out faster and not be pressured by salespeople, it is important to recognize that the do-it-yourself world has its drawbacks, particularly for manufacturers.

In addition to your message getting lost inside the store, another issue with self-service is that there is no opportunity to uncover emerging trends or explore purchase drivers. If customers walk into the store, shop, and leave without speaking to a single human being, how will the stores and manufacturers test the desirability of their brands or products? A store's own point-of-sale data are great for learning what was sold, but what do they tell you about what wasn't sold? Not a thing. So what is a manufacturer or retailer to do? Learn how to communicate with the consumer by way of sales associates or direct feedback research.

That said, merging with Sears allowed Kmart to differentiate itself from the other top two discounters: Wal-Mart and Target. Now Kmart can feature its popular private-label brands, such as Martha Stewart Everyday, Joe Boxer, and Jaclyn Smith, in traditional shopping malls that house Sears department stores. This additional real estate represents a huge opportunity for Kmart, since over 52 percent of the customers who shop in malls also shop at discount stores. When Kmart's brands are put in Sears' aisles, a whole new crop of customers who in the past skipped making a separate trip to Kmart will be exposed to the merchandise. Meanwhile, Kmart's typical blue-collar customer will now come in contact with Sears' more upscale brands, such as Lands' End.

GOT MILK?

I'd like to share an interesting example that underscores the critical importance of connecting with the consumer and demonstrates the degree to which a connection can be made. In this case it wasn't just one company that missed its chance to reach its market base; it was an entire industry.

The panty hose business has been declining for nine consecutive years. This is due in part to the emergence of business casual dressing and an overall trend of women moving away from wearing panty hose altogether. Worse yet, the trend has been accelerated by the very retailers that are selling the product. Seeing the decline in sales, retailers decided that they should cut back on the amount of product and move the floor space that had been devoted to panty hose elsewhere in the store. However, the retailers made a misstep when they eliminated the variety of colors and styles they carried. Although young adults don't purchase panty hose to the same extent that the adult market does, they do purchase colors and novelty panty hose. Over the last eight years retailers gave younger consumers even less incentive to think about panty hose as they entered their career years. Thus, the industry missed its chance to cultivate a new generation of users as they entered the age when they would even think about the product. The manufacturers did not change the dynamics, and the business continued to drop 5 to 10 percent a year.

Fueling the decline in the panty hose industry was the introduction of enhanced products from skin-care companies such as Jergens, which began marketing products that promised the shimmer of panty hose with the comfort of bare legs. They also offered products that competed head-on with the benefits of panty hose, such as firming agents and skin tone correctors.

So how did the panty hose industry respond? It did virtually nothing. One person did attempt to stand up for the hosiery industry. The president of the Hosiery Association embarked on a mission to force Jergens to remove the words "panty hose" from its ad campaigns. Although she was successful in that effort, was it really enough? When I asked several manufacturers what they planned to do about this situation, they felt they didn't have the resources to address the problem. The panty hose business should have taken a lesson from the Dairy Association.

Almost everyone has seen the incredibly visible "Got Milk?" campaign. Most of us might think it was a very successful effort because of the level of awareness it achieved, but did it really help sell more milk? Not really: Milk sales didn't increase during the campaign. However, the industry kept its market share, and that was a real accomplishment with increased competition from the rise in popularity of carbonated soft drinks, one of the fastest growing categories in the food industry, as well as flavored teas, bottled water, and other soft drinks. The exposure that resulted from that very well executed and stylized campaign protected the industry's current consumer base and prevented pending declines. Thus, if sales growth is the only measure you use for success, think again. By using the "Got Milk?" campaign, the Dairy Association was able to effectively, though at great expense, protect its space. I bet they'd tell you it was worth every penny.

What are you doing to protect your space? What are you doing to educate consumers about the benefits of your product? What is your industry or business doing to support the growth or space you currently have?

I DON'T GIVE A DAMN ABOUT MY REPUTATION

With your brand message now being heard loud and clear by customers, it is critical to back up that message with a stellar reputation. We live in a world where consumer opinion can be shared with the masses via blogs and other word-of-mouth channels. This reality requires you to look at how you market your product or brand because that goes deeper than just the images you think your customers

> I measure success by the ability to communicate your message. Success is something that you earn, gain, or protect.

want to see, both reinforcing your brand's reputation and tapping into the aspirations and behaviors of your audience. Communicating your brand image is still key—and is probably more important to teen consumers up to a point—but marketing and advertising campaigns need to delve deeper and reflect the attributes most prized by a brand's customers.

It's essential that managers rethink how the integrity of their brand is communicated, whether that is done through actual customer testimonials, celebrity endorsements, or partnerships with brands that have the same interests. Don't sell the consumers with superficial images; instead, explore the attributes that drive their behavior and educate them about how your brand meets their goals and aspirations. Let's take a closer look at how this is done.

A PICTURE IS WORTH A THOUSAND WORDS

Every day we are exposed to thousands of images that either take root in our subconscious or are forgotten immediately. Most of us can recall only a handful of the ad images we see on any particular day. Advertising, whether in print or broadcast, is an essential strategy for communicating the existence of a brand and establishing that brand's message and reputation. Wouldn't it make sense to ensure that the images associated with your brand are unique and differentiate your products and services from those of the competition?

This is why I constantly am amazed at the barrage of advertisements from competing companies that sound and look the same and, while offering something enticing to look at, do not reflect a brand's message and have nothing to do with the product they are selling. I first began noticing this

Image advertising is valuable only if it differentiates your brand from the competition and taps into your customers' conscious and unconscious needs.

in the fragrance industry. An ad for one popular fragrance featured a young model lying on the beach, the water lapping up and causing her white blouse, which was tied loosely over her swimsuit, to look transparent. I wondered what that had to do with fragrance. Just a few days later I saw a competitor's ad showing almost the same image. I had to double-check to make sure they weren't the same brand. I don't recall either brand now, and so you can see how effective that marketing strategy was.

This was not just an aberration; it continues to happen over and over across industries. You can open almost any fashion magazine and see ads that make the same mistakes, portraying images that are completely disconnected with the consumer and are used by direct competitors. I don't know about you, but if I spent a lot of money on an ad campaign, I'd want to be able to get some form of brand recognition from it. I don't expect everyone to remember every advertisement he or she sees, but I do expect that consumers should be able to retain some of the ads they see and relate the ad to the product, especially when it's *my* product and *my* advertising budget.

How is it possible for consumers to identify with ads and retain the brand's or product's name when the images used are all so similar? A more important question is, In light of what we know about the aspirational motivations for consumer spending, how are consumers going to relate to these products when the brands are not communicating the benefits of the products? I am not suggesting that ads should forgo using imagery. What I am saying is that an ad should have its own personality and communicate the essence of the brand through its images, that those images make a statement that will give it an immediate identity to the consumer. This misuse of image advertising isn't unique to the fragrance industry; it's found across business sectors in ads for hotels, sportswear, car rentals, and many other products and services.

Brands need to connect with consumers and educate them on why they should invest in a particular product or service. Ad campaigns that connect with the emotions of the consumer are a start, but that connection has to be authentic—it has to deliver on the promise. And the brands have to be able to separate themselves from the competition.

The Dairy Association with its "Got Milk?" campaign, Geico, Ralph Lauren, and Calvin Klein are all examples of companies that established a look for their brands, like it or not, and communicated a consistent, clear message to consumers.

USE THE MEDIA TO TELL YOUR STORY

The media world is bursting at the seams, with more cable channels, news programs, magazines, newspapers, news-letters, and online publications than ever before. And the media are hungry for anything new that will appeal to their

> Brands need to educate consumers about which product or service they should invest in.

viewers' interests. We know that the majority of consumers are short on time and use the media to learn about new products, services, and techniques. They watch infomercials and other paid programming, do Google searches, or Ask Jeeves; they read articles and keep an eye on the national and cable news programs to find out about the right product or service to buy or invest in, depending on their needs and interests: Have $100, make a fortune with Forex, or lose 85 pounds in 10 months like these good folks.

George Foreman breathed new life into an infant industry with his line of indoor grills. The product was introduced via an infomercial and captured the viewer's attention by featuring a celebrity whose very livelihood was based on being a heavyweight but who had found his way to health and fitness. NPD's Kitchen Audit tracked indoor grills in American homes and found that with the introduction of the George Foreman grill, ownership of indoor grills went from 11 percent of the population 1993 to about 40 percent in 2002.

What I'm trying to tell you is to *use the media* to introduce your brand and its message. As with the George Foreman grill, there are countless examples of well-executed marketing strategies that pair a product that has tremendous consumer appeal with the right images and then use the media to maximize its exposure.

Cleaning is a chore most people would like to do less of. Procter & Gamble, which knows a thing or two about household cleaning, came up with a great product that tapped into the idea that consumers could reduce the time they spent cleaning. Enter the Swiffer, a disposable "wipe" that draws dust to it and makes dusting seem easier. Their catchphrase was: "Stop Cleaning. Get Swiffer." When they coupled this simple message with an adaptation of Devo's

> Use the media to reinforce your brand image and spread your message.

"Whip It" in television spots, the product became a huge success. And if consumers could elevate their lifestyles by spending less time dusting, then, logically, they could really elevate it by spending less time scrubbing and washing floors. Enter Swiffer Wet and Swiffer WetJet, product extensions that appealed with the same "elevation" messages; both were both huge success stories for P&G.

What we are seeing is a new dimension to advertising and product marketing. Swiffer is hitting the core elements of anyone who cleans or provides the products for someone to use for cleaning. The willingness of the consumer to try this product is multiplied by the number of people who not only relate to the marketing message but pass it along through word of mouth. People love to tell me how much they adore their Swiffer. They are excited when I demonstrate or point out the new products Swiffer has launched. There is something happening here that is quite clear and certainly worthy of being picked up on by any brand or retailer. Sure, it would be nice to have a product that is so connected to consumers' emotions, but would you think a cleaning product that still requires you to clean would have this kind of emotional connection? Now, if the cleaning product market can do it, so can your market.

Another great example of connecting with the consumer is Gillette's Trac II Plus razor. The acceptance of this product was amazing. The Trac II Plus featured the use of two blades, and commercials and ads demonstrated the ability of the second blade to get a hair before it has a chance to recede. What the first blade misses, the second blade can get. Sounds great and promises a closer, more comfortable shave. Now add in the lubricant strip at the point of contact with the skin on the cartridge housing the blades and you have an even more smooth and comfortable shave. Others copied Gillette and developed their own twin-blade systems. Did Gillette stop there? No, it introduced the Mach 3 and then the Mach 3 Turbo and then the M3 Power. The Mach 3 boasted that "three heads are better than two." And the M3 Power put a little vibrating action into the shave to make shaving an even closer and more rewarding experience. Is there a Mach 4 or Mach 5 in our future? Who knows? But with Gillette recently merging with Procter & Gamble, we can be reasonably sure that they will continue to find ways to elevate the shaving experience and communicate their products' abilities very effectively to the consumer. Educate. Elevate. What is happening is that innovation alone is no longer enough to get a product to sell. Education through marketing is what gets the message across, and that's what entices consumers to purchase products.

Whatever your product or brand may be, the important thing is *not* to BOGO it. If you take the time to explore what your customers want and develop your product to meet their needs, you're almost there. If you then educate the consumers about what your product can do for them—how it can elevate them in some way—you very likely will have a success on your hands. Your message, just like your product and your brand, is your responsibility. Understand the terms that mean something to your customer, use them, and see what happens when you do.

3

WE FINALLY GOT
A PIECE OF THE PIE

WHEN I MEET WITH PROFESSIONAL MARKETERS and managers across industries, there is a general insistence that the brands they sell fall within three categories: private label, designer, and national brands (see Fig. 3-1). These three segments are an outdated convention of the sales industry, and if you believe that they are the only types of brands your customers are interested in, you're in trouble. When I ask consumers to describe the types of brands they are loyal to, they look at products across the six categories featured in Fig. 3-2.

As the consumer's needs, wants, and desires have become increasingly multifaceted, we are seeing an expansion of brand categories. The traditional designer, national, and private label segments have spawned three new categories: private, licensed, and entertainment brands.

FIGURE 3-1 Brand mix profile of the traditional way that product brands are viewed.

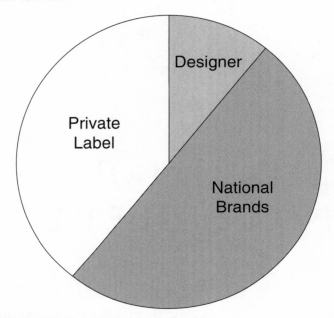

SOURCE: *Beyond the Data with Marshal Cohen.*

Further refining your brand's characteristics and knowing the intricacies of your particular category are essential to keeping up with the changing profile of consumers who are in pursuit of any one of a variety of aspirational experiences. In deciding what to buy and how to buy it, consumers clearly are looking for opportunities to upgrade their lifestyles. This trend is influencing the way businesses conceive of and create new offerings, the means by which a brand is communicated so that core customers are not ignored while a whole new audience's interest is enticed, and the method by which an offering is distributed and sold. The problem here is that the way individuals believe they can better themselves is unknowable. How do you determine the aspirational motivations of your customers and identify the elements that satisfy

FIGURE 3-2   **The new brand mix profile.**

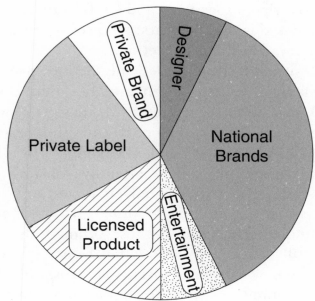

SOURCE: *Beyond the Data with Marshal Cohen.*

this behavior? Right now, the world of entertainment holds tremendous sway over brand loyalty and purchasing decisions. We'll be examining this trend later in this chapter.

WE'RE UP TO SIX

Let's look at the traditional brand categories: private label, designer, and national.

The private label category describes generic brands with products sold in nondescript packaging: the plain white box, brown wrapper, or packaging with the store's logo. This category has been replaced almost completely by private brands, an offshoot that is credited for the success of discounters such as Target, Wal-Mart, and Kmart as well as manufacturers that include Kenmore, which was manufactured by Whirlpool for Sears, and Craftsman Tools, which was created and is sold by Sears. I'll discuss private brands in greater detail in the next section.

The designer category practically defines itself: Think Calvin Klein, Elizabeth Arden and her Red Door, and Jaguar. What's new here is the way the designer model has been affected by the phenomenon of the thinning middle, which I'll cover in greater detail in Chapter 5. Briefly, high-end brands are being sought after by consumers at all income levels. This has created an opportunity for discounters to invest in private brands as well as other licensed and entertainment brands. Although the designer category still exists in its traditional form, it has helped generate the new categories discussed below.

National brands continue to emphasize value and quality. They're priced more reasonably than designer brands are and both the quality of the product and the retail experience are better than those of the lower-priced brands. The challenge that national brands and the businesses that sell them have is the changing marketplace dynamic that is edging them out. In the next few chapters you'll learn about emerging market trends, such as the thinning middle, lifestyle segmentation, and the Sea of Sameness, that are making it difficult (though not impossible) for national brands to compete. Levi-Strauss found a way to differentiate itself among midsector brands and compete with designer labels.

The 100-year-old company developed a high-end product for the low-end market by creating a Levi Signature brand that appealed to consumers looking to elevate their jeans purchases. In essence, they refined their products and branding message to appeal to the lower-end market

(Wal-Mart's core audience) with upmarket offerings. Levi-Strauss understood the dynamic among consumers that had propelled Target to its level of success: The perception of affluence is critical to the consumer, who now counts this element as part of the overall value equation of an offering or brand. (You'll learn more about the value equation in the next chapter.) Reaching this level of realization and redefining core aspects of its business and product line was not a seamless process, however, as Levi suffered through a variety of missteps, such as the "funny leg" commercials and other off-point ad campaigns. Yet, as they came to understand the hidden desires of their marketplace and as customers themselves became more aware of this behavioral trend, the company's plan fell into place.

THE OFFSHOOTS

In this section we'll look at the brand categories that have resulted from changes in customer behavior, market dynamics, and the retail landscape.

Private brands grew out of the private label category; the term refers to the creation of a brand name around a generic product. This approach offers the allure of a designer label at a bargain price. Target's primary growth lies in this category, with the discounter selling both designer and in some cases fictitious designer brands. Fictitious brands come from fabricated people and places. Haagen-Dazs, for example, is not a place, a person, or even a thing, but does that change my perception of the ice cream? In all my years I have yet to say no to a scoop. But on the other side of the equation, do consumers perceive its value as higher because of the exotic name? You bet they do. Fig. 3-3 shows the private label mix profile.

FIGURE 3-3   Private label mix profile.

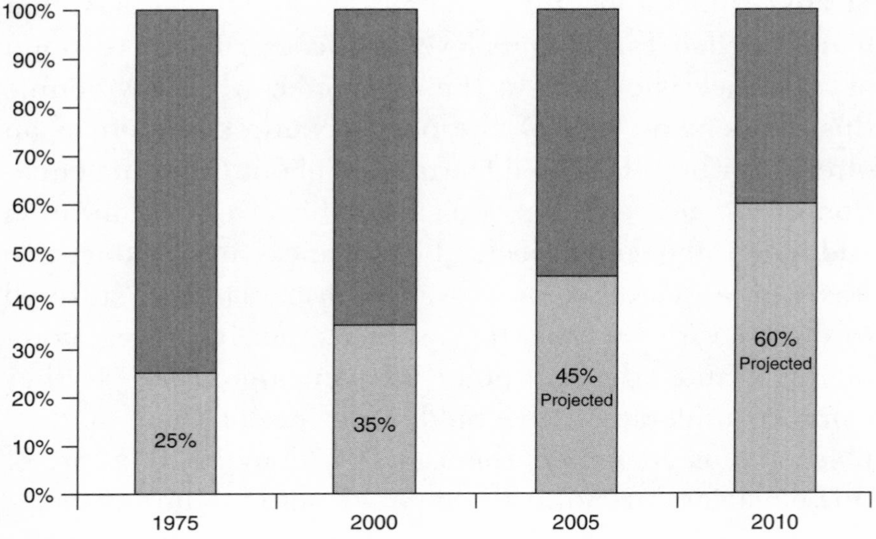

SOURCE: NPD Fashionworld Consumer.

JC Penney has done a terrific job at marketing its own brands, particularly Stafford, a private label men's wear product that has become a private brand for the retailer. JC Penney markets this brand as if it were any other national brand its stores carry, and Stafford has grown to become a brand that consumers rate very high for awareness and even more for quality and fit. JC Penney takes great pride in delivering a better-than-expected product that the consumer will be inclined to become loyal to and spread the word about. The way the brand is approached is similar to that of a designer or national brand. It is not designed to be lower-priced; it is designed to have greater value. And JC Penney delivers on that intention. The Stafford brand ranks among the top four brands that have high consumer loyalty and intent to repurchase. As was mentioned earlier, Target has designer-oriented private label programs, but consumers don't perceive them to be private label products. They see brands such as C9 athletic apparel by Champion and Danskin Freestyle, both made for Target designer wear, as private brands. And these proprietary brands are just that: private brands. They have the look and feel of other national brands but are products that are designed and marketed for a specific retailer. This approach extends to all types of consumer products, from fashion to sports equipment and even electronics.

One of my favorite examples of private branding and the success that comes from building a private label product offering into a private brand is Kenmore. I remember one summer when I worked in a laundry service center. I learned firsthand that Whirlpool was making the washing machines for Sears under the Kenmore label. I couldn't believe it. I learned that these machines were so similar that it didn't pay to buy a name brand; it really paid to buy the less expensive Kenmore brand. Since then things have changed somewhat as private label and private brands have gone into buying direct from other factories, not only the ones that make the branded products.

One of my most amazing discoveries happened when I went to visit the Titleist golf ball factory. I watched the production line and wondered why the balls that were coming out of the machines and heading to the branding station— the point where they emboss the name and number on the ball—were not being separated from the ones that were getting XXXed. For those of you who don't play golf, there are golf balls you can buy that have XXX stamped on top of the brand name of the ball. This mark is supposed to indicate that the golf balls are either used or not quite up to standard in some way.

When I asked the production supervisor how they knew the difference between the first-quality balls and the XXXed-out ones, he stated that there was no difference. They had an order for XXXed-out ones and didn't have enough seconds lying around, and so they just printed them that way and shipped them to the stores in clear plastic blister packs rather than in fancy boxes with four sleeves and three golf balls in each sleeve. I arrived home from that trip realizing that the golf balls I had been buying were no different from the ones that cost about half as much. I also realized that no matter what the ball was, XXXed-out or not, hitting it straight was still one of the toughest things I would ever love to hate.

Now, don't think that all XXXed-out golf balls are top quality. This occurs only when they don't have an ample supply of true seconds to ship. I asked about that too. I was informed that the demand for discounted golf balls far exceeds the supply of blemished golf balls, and so the odds are pretty high in our favor for getting first-quality balls at discounted prices. Besides, do you really think most people would be able to recognize a slightly defective golf ball? It might even help cure all those slices by compensating for the error in my swing.

Private brands continue to be a strong category but one that requires a more significant commitment on the part of the firm. These are high-end brands that represent resource-intensive business initiatives. The business must own the brand completely and commit to making sure that the brand message, product offerings, marketing approach, and distribution network are at the highest level of effectiveness. More important, the private brand absolutely must reflect the core attributes and maintain the image of the primary business.

> Branding is what makes the consumer associate himself
> or herself with the product. Branding gives the product
> personality and image and, even more important, gives
> the consumer something to share with others.

Licensed product, along with entertainment brands, represents the most significant change in brand thinking. Emerging out of the national brand piece of the pie, licensed product is not the same as branded product coming from the original manufacturer with logos (e.g., Lacoste's alligator) added. Smart businesses are aligning themselves with companies that have an existing and, more important, a *recognizable* brand identity and buying a license to use their logos. Sports associations such as Major League Baseball and the National Basketball Association are obvious examples of branded businesses or organizations that license out their images. What's new about this trend is how it increasingly is linked to the appeal of the entertainment industry in all its various forms.

Consumer behavior is affected, whether consciously or subconsciously, by what consumers see on the street, in films, and on television, at the theater, and across myriad entertainment channels. West Coast Customs came to prominence in the MTV program "Pimp My Ride," an ersatz makeover show for 18- to 22- year-olds with cars that need serious upgrading. The garage is California's p remiere automotive restyling center and was a closely held secret among hip-hop's most prominent stars. The garage's "street cred" is undeniable, but the show, hosted by the hip-hop star Xzibit, boosted West Coast Customs' exposure and entertainment value. A licensing bonanza ensued, with everything from T-shirts to skateboards to model cars displaying the West Coast Customs logo being produced. With over 72 million viewers and growing, licensing out this now very visible and powerful logo was a smart business decision.

Consumer electronics has latched on to this proven formula as well, licensing the images of today's hottest sports figures, artists, and actors for use in video games and using those images as brands to sell their products. Games in the Def Jam line are a particularly good example of this approach, using the Def Jam name and logo along with the images of its signed artists to create market appeal. Can you guess how many licensing deals are in the works for the latest *Star Wars* movie, *The Revenge of the Sith*? There are 400 in over 30 countries for thousands of products. You've got burgers, ring tones, toys, video games, T-shirts—the list goes on and on. Since its original release in 1977, Star Wars merchandise has racked up about $9 billion in retail sales, almost three times as much as the combined box office sales of $3.4 billion for the series. It's expected that the licensing deals for *Sith* will bring in another $1.5 billion. (See http://news.yahoo.com/s/nm/20050518/film_nm/star-wars_merchandise_dc_2.)

Related to licensing is the creation of entertainment brands. The insatiable appetite of consumers for all things famous has been a significant factor in business development, brand messaging, and marketing strategies. Paris Hilton has her own line of clothes; Jessica Simpson, cosmetics; and Phat Farm and Russell Simmons, music and fashion. Daisy Fuentes is at Kohls; Jaclyn Smith is at Kmart, Shaquille O'Neal has several lines; the Olsen twins are at Wal-Mart; and Ty Pennington is at Sears Home.

Let's consider Jennifer Lopez for a moment: She is a multidimensional brand. JLo is able to market herself as an

WHEN ENTERTAINMENT BRANDS GO TOO FAR

When brands become so commercialized that they lose their edge, they can lose their loyal customers as well. When Fubu became the rage of suburbia, it lost its way. Many urban wear stores that seek to remain true to their core customers will do so by seeking out new brands, and current urban lines such as Sean John will have to reinvent themselves and create looks that say urban, not suburban.

actress, a singer, a model, a fragrance, and an apparel line. But whichever product she is marketing, it is the power of the celebrity that makes it all about a lifestyle, not just a product. This celebrity-based product carries a built-in consumer following and lifestyle identity. As this trend continues, it could create a backlash if these brands don't pay close attention to the integrity of the brand. Celebrity brands are encroaching on the designer space in many cases, and the consumer is willing to support this trend, but only if the celebrity is maintaining the appropriate profile and the product remains worthy. Figs. 3-4 and 3-5 indicate the increase in sales of licensed and nonlicensed toys and video games between 2002 and 2004.

THE POWER OF CELEBRITY

The significant corporate investment that businesses are making in celebrity endorsements supports our finding that entertainment is the number one growing influencer of

FIGURE 3-4 Licensed versus nonlicensed: dollar sales percentages for traditional toys.

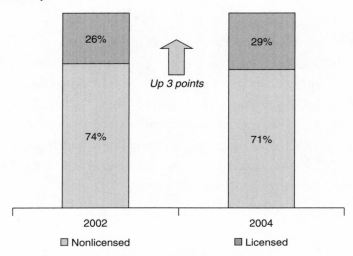

SOURCE: NPD Group/NPD Funworld/Consumer Panel.

FIGURE 3-5 Licensed versus nonlicensed: dollar sales percentages for video games (including hardware, software, and accessories).

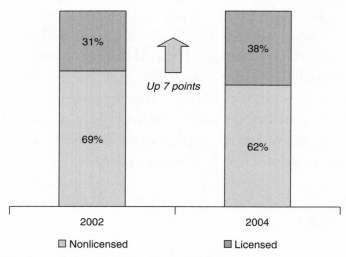

SOURCE: NPD Group/NPD Funworld/Point-of-Sale.

consumer behavior today. In just three years' time, celebrity influence on apparel purchases for consumers has jumped 300 percent. In 2001, 3 percent of consumers stated that celebrities had an influence on their apparel purchases. In 2004, that number jumped to 9 percent. Although this doesn't sound like a lot, consider that the apparel business represents the number one purchase involving discretionary spending among consumers and that apparel is also the number one gift item at holiday time. In light of the fact that in 2004 Americans spent $173 billion on apparel, this small percentage equals a significant net dollar amount.

Ideally, the appeal of a celebrity, whether it is based on physical attributes, lifestyle, or accomplishments, will succeed in attracting new customers to the brand. However, committing to a celebrity spokesperson is not without risks. Remember Mike Tyson and his wife Robin Givens drinking Pepsi? That ad lost all its appeal after the boxer was accused of spousal abuse. And what about those deals that ultimately get canceled: Converse dropped Dennis Rodman because of the NBA player's bad behavior and antics on and off the court; Kobe Bryant lost his McDonald's deal among others after being indicted for sexual assault; and Pepsi dropped Ludacris after Bill O'Reilly of Fox News voiced his outrage about the deal, taking the rapper to task for his profane lyrics. Then you have those celebrities who drop out of the public eye for a period of time. I recall the launch of a fragrance bearing the name of Céline Dion. This new fragrance did well but almost fell from the public's awareness after the singer's sudden retirement. When Dion came out of retirement with a new album on the charts, the fragrance came right back to the forefront just in time for the holiday selling season.

Some campaigns are very effective in getting consumers to relate to a brand just by having a celebrity associated

with it. In some cases it is the lifestyle of the celebrity that
is appealing to the consumer. Take Madonna, for example:
What does she stand for in the consumer's mind?   Some
love the idea that she was the ultimate bad girl. Some love
the fact that she is the ultimate example of a grown-up living in the not-so-grown-up world. You thought I was going
to say material world; well, you were close. Madonna per-
sonifies the complex life of consumers: She's a mother and
a sex symbol; she's over 40, yet her style transcends age;
she's a pop icon and a spiritual disciple. As Madonna continues to redefine herself, she will continue to appeal to a
broad cross section of consumers who admire aspects of
her professional and personal life and aspire to reach their
own goals.

A leading apparel specialty retailer hit a huge home run
with the actress Sara Jessica Parker and is a prime example
of a company that understands exactly who its customers
are and selects a spokesperson who will appeal to them.
The holiday season 2004 campaign introduced Sara Jessica
Parker as the company's new spokesperson in a series of
advertisements on television, in print, and on its website.
Consumers would visit the retailer's website, be able to mix
and match over a hundred possible combinations of outfits, and either purchase online or download the image and
bring it into a store to be able to try it on. In a majority of
the cases, the image the consumer brought into the store
was the image with Sarah Jessica Parker. Despite the hundreds of options the consumers had, they still wanted to
look like SJP. Now, was it that that outfit was so much
more appealing than all the others? Or was it that the consumer really was being influenced by the image and
lifestyle the celebrity portrayed? Experience tells us that it
was the latter.

4

FORMULATING YOUR VALUE EQUATION

ONSUMERS TODAY think multiple times before making a purchase. They ask themselves how badly they want an item, whether they need it, whether the price might go down if they wait to make the purchase, and, if so, how important it is to them to have the item now as opposed to buying it later for less. When I speak to consumers, they tell me how they constantly wrestle with these questions. What their final decision is reflects the aspects of the brand and product that are the most valuable to them. Although consumers cite value as the most important factor influencing their purchases, how do you determine what they actually *mean*, and how do you create a message that taps into a customer's unique perception of value?

Some customers define value as everyday low prices, others define it as a great product with lots of features, and

The Value Equation

The value equation reflects how your customer assesses and prioritizes the four elements of value: style, price, quality, and service. What is the trade-off for your customers?

others tell you that value is the way the brand meets their needs and desires. Whatever the definition, it is clear that there are four key elements that constitute value.

Value is the combination of style, price, quality, and service, and consumers are willing to give up some components to get more of others. In marketing your brand it is important to understand how you communicate the four components of the value equation. You need to recognize what those components are, how your product and brand address them, and how you communicate your value equation to the customer.

You don't have to excel in each component. This means that you may minimize service in the equation but will have to compensate in other areas to offset that. Thus, selling a pair of shoes without service is quite acceptable if the styles offered are strong, prices are fair or better than fair, and quality is right in line. Designer Shoe Warehouse (DSW) is a great example of this. By offering self-service, easy-to-find sizing, and a wide assortment of top name and current styles, DSW offers great savings with little service. The consumer clearly accepts this, and even consumers who are used to shopping in stores that offer high levels of service in footwear are finding it a challenge to ignore this competitor.

> It's your job to figure out just what it is about your brand and product that consumers will find valuable.

FIRST IMPRESSIONS: STYLE

When consumers choose to make a purchase, they are deciding whether the product is worth the money, whether they really need the product, whether the product can be purchased elsewhere or later on for less money, and whether the act of making the purchase is worth the effort. They also are deciding if the way the product looks fits their image or lifestyle.

There are a lot of questions that pop into a consumer's mind when he or she first is considering a purchase. Yet the reality is that consumers give a product almost one-quarter of a second of thought when they shop. That's right: one-quarter of a second. In that fraction of a second, consumers decide if they will read the package, compare it to other similar products, and determine if this is the product for them.

What can you do to turn that quarter of a second into more time and hence a more thoughtful effort by the customer? The very brand and product you are marketing can be used to extend the decision-making process. When you look at your product—and, more important, your brand

> Customers form an impression of a product in no more than a quarter of a second.

message as conveyed by the product's packaging—is the connection to your customer apparent? Does your package tell buyers what your product will do for them? Does it make the product jump out at them? The next time you are in the grocery store, take a look at the toothpaste aisle and consider two things: color and connection. Look at how the brands are trying to make their products stand out to convey a message. Whether they have whiteners, fluoride, crystals, or even baking soda, they are all telling the consumer in that quarter of a second what makes their brand different.

> The marketing message for enhanced products such as denim that doesn't get wet or stained and clothes that don't fade and change color when exposed to sunlight is communicated immediately through the style or package.

The way your brand connects with your customers is the beginning of the brand's value equation. Package design is where that connection takes full form: Your packaging must convey the aspects that create value for that product. Soft drink companies do a wonderful job of using their packages as a means to differentiate their product, communicate its benefits, and give customers a reason to buy it in the first place. They've created collectible designs as well as seasonal packaging, and they've learned how to communicate special promotional opportunities right on the can or bottle.

Now make it snappy. You have about a quarter of a second. Go!

IS IT WORTH IT: PRICE

Price has always been an important component in selling one's product, but this aspect has become even more important as we have entered into a phase in consumer purchase behavior that is unique to the times. Consumers today assess every purchase they make. Even those who are the most carefree in their spending are beginning to think twice about what they are paying for their purchases, and the majority of consumers are basing their decisions on cost and necessity.

Do I really need this? Is it at the right price, and will I be able to get it for less if I wait a week or two? Is this the best value for my dollar? These are the questions consumers ask themselves before making a purchase. Consumers who just see and buy without thinking are rare, and it goes deeper than that, with many consumers feeling compelled to justify their purchasing decisions. Because of this justification process, there is a mandate to understand the elements that go into the consumer's thinking when it comes to price.

This issue can be demonstrated best in the way consumers shop for technology. Almost everyone has the experience of buying an electronic item and then, in a very short period of time, seeing that item or something similar come down in price to the point where one has to justify the price that one paid by referring to the time one has had it in one's possession or used it. DVD players are a great example of this.

In 2001 the average price of a DVD player was about $200. In 2004 the average price fell to $85. If you bought one before the year 1995, you were likely to pay close to $1,000. In consumer electronics, as products mature and move toward becoming commodities, the price usually plummets. Thus, in the customers' minds there is a price point at which they are willing to spend for the item. When the retail price reaches that point, they buy it. Early adopters aside—those who *have* to be the "first kid on the block"—most consumers are willing to do their homework, shop around, and wait for the price point to come to them. All other components of the value equation being equal, price is often the deciding factor, particularly in consumer electronics, household appliances, sporting goods (such as golf clubs), outdoor grills, and of course trendy apparel.

THIS WILL LAST FOREVER: QUALITY

The third part of the value equation is the consumer's assessment of quality. Is this brand the highest in quality? Is this the level of quality that matches my standard? Does the level of quality suggest something about my own standards? Brands that convey a certain standard of living and help customers aspire to that standard have a strong foundation for expanding their portfolio of products as well as their customer base.

John Deere, a brand that has 92 percent brand awareness and a sterling reputation for quality, recently expanded its focus from tractors and farm equipment to include the do-it-yourself homeowner for lawn tractors and even other product categories. The company naturally was concerned that the integrity of its core customer (the commercial farm and landscape professional) might be jeopardized by offering a lawn tractor at stores such as Home Depot, but that has proved not to be the case. In fact, John Deere's heritage that has endured generation after generation has made the jump to this new market, so much so

> Brands that convey a certain standard of living and help users aspire to that standard are better positioned to expand their range of offerings and grow their customer base.

that it actually is considered a cool brand by the youth market seeking out John Deere hats and T-shirts.

John Deere has demonstrated the ability to take its brand beyond its core product mix and widen its distribution to include new target users and distribution outlets, and the company did it all while maintaining the essence of its brand values. John Deere successfully extended its reputation for quality in farm and professional landscaping equipment to the home lawn mower market.

Another great example of the quality component is our love for fast food. What does fast food have in common with quality? you ask. A lot. Just a short time ago McDonald's—and the whole fast-food industry—was having a tough go. Sales were down, and the future looked gloomy. McDonald's used a few E's and figured it out. They spent time and energy exploring what the customer wanted. They learned that healthy foods were the issue, or in their case, the perception of the lack of healthy foods on their menu. Between high fat content, carbohydrate counting, and "supersizing," fast food wasn't looking like the best way to feed a family. People, especially mothers, were trying to find a healthier option for eating out.

McDonald's added milk, juices, and fruit along with soda and salads to the burgers on the menu, and not only did they get the moms and kids back, they suddenly were selling higher-priced product: salads selling for $5 versus

Big Macs for $3! Mothers wanted to eat healthier, still get the convenience of fast food, and feel that they were getting good-quality food. McDonald's bounced back. Its "Happy Meals" program is still going strong, and between the gift with the purchase and the new menu focus on women, McDonald's is once again the gold standard in fast food.

At the corporate level McDonald's is a great example of a brand that utilizes the Five E's of marketing:

1. They Educate internally on what customers want and externally by telling customers that they have healthy alternatives: milk and juices instead of sodas, salads instead of burgers, and veggies instead of fries.

2. They Entertain with the connection to kids through Happy Meal toys, tie-in promotions with new movies and other entertainment properties, the use of Ronald in their marketing, and the development of Playland "kids only" areas designed to keep the kids happy while they're there.

3. They continuously Explore new and innovative ways to connect with the use of new interactive menus that offer a wider view of the menu instead of just words on a light box. They also are exploring brands to partner with, such as Newman's Own salad dressings for their salads.

4. They are Elevating the customers by offering healthier choices and allowing them to elevate their families or themselves by living a healthier lifestyle while saving money and time eating at their restaurants.

5. They continue to Evaluate their approach and make adjustments as needed.

In terms of its value equation, McDonald's delivers more for the money, better choices, and healthier living and lets the customer have fun while doing it. They long ago established a consistent level of quality that the consumer can always expect from one McDonald's to another, without exception. Whether the counter person asks if you want fries with that, well, that's not a quality issue—that's service.

SERVICE WITH A SMILE

The service aspect of the equation is a tricky one because consumers are not always consciously aware of their own expectations. We've already talked about self-service shopping, but another trend in the do-it-yourself market is ready-to-assemble furniture. Consumers shop for these items in huge self-service stores where they can see the furniture assembled, haul away the (often) very heavy kits, get it all home somehow, and spend the day assembling the furniture themselves. What figures into the value equation here is a modicum of style, a great price, decent quality, and virtually no service whatsoever. But that last item often doesn't even occur to the consumers until they're trying to load everything into the car and realizing that they're completely on their own and not nearly as strong as they thought they were. Two great examples of retailers that understand the value of service are auto dealers and luxury stores.

AUTO SERVICE

Auto dealers operate on very tight margins and constantly explore ways to build customer loyalty. One way to improve margins *and* loyalty was to improve service operations. They can't compete on price with discount service centers, but there *are* things they can offer that the discounters can't. Thus, dealerships are extending their service to include new features such as a personal service technician who will be the customer's primary contact. If customers can't wait for their cars, loaners often are supplied so that they can get to work and pick up their cars later. For customers who prefer to wait, waiting rooms have been transformed into "lounges" equipped with a color television, magazines, doughnuts, and fresh coffee. All this is being done to help car owners feel that they are getting more service, comfort, and attention while paying a bit more for the service they are getting. By extending service beyond the core task of auto repair and maintenance, auto dealers can compete with discount service centers and hold on to their customers longer.

LUXURY STORES

In the department store world Nordstrom's has set itself above the rest in several ways. Nordstrom's built its reputation as it expanded in the 1990s and into the 2000s with its exceptional service component. Besides sending birthday cards to customers and occasionally having sales associates drop products off at customers' homes, it even developed the "concierge" as a service that few stores would think to offer. The concierge is not just an information desk; it's a person dedicated to giving the customer personal assistance, whether it's helping to figure out what kind of gift to buy, where the stemware can be found, or how to get a new clothing purchase altered quickly. The value of the concierge is immeasurable in making the consumer feel important, and this relationship goes far in creating customer loyalty and word-of-mouth endorsements. What it did to help establish Nordstrom's as a brand was priceless as well.

Nordstrom's does one other really great thing: It has dedicated the precious floor space in the rotunda, that space between the escalators in the center of the store, to entertaining the nonshopper with a cluster of comfortable lounge chairs and even, on certain days, a piano player. Now women can shop knowing that their husbands are sitting comfortably in the rotunda, people watching, napping, or listening to the music. Women shop more, and more comfortably, and husbands don't stand around outside fitting rooms holding handbags in that special way that says "No, it's *not* mine!" Again, if you can't compete on price, your service, quality, or style had better be making up for it in some way. Nordstrom's found a successful formula for the value equation, and the way the company did it involved that letter E we keep talking about.

FORMULATE YOUR OWN VALUE EQUATION

Take a good look at your own business. Evaluate your existing service operation and explore how you can serve your customers better. Can you service the customer in a way that may not even be directly related to the service or product you offer? Can you entertain through coffee or other amenities? Car dealers had to explore and educate themselves on what it was that the consumer was getting outside and address it head-on. If price is not going to be the fix, the brand needs to do something different to balance out the value equation. Emphasize the components of the equation that highlight the benefit of your product or service and educate your customers so that they know the advantages of your offering. Most important, keep evaluating how your service operation is performing: That's going to tell you things about your customers, and your (satisfied) customers are going to tell others about you.

5

THE THINNING MIDDLE

THE COMPLICATED PROFILE of the "average" customer isn't the only phenomenon managers have to deal with. Although it's quite an accomplishment to create a product, brand, and message that will resonate with your customer and create a lifelong relationship, it doesn't help you *grow* your business. Yes, it *sustains* it, but the question facing all businesses, particularly those that deal in high-volume, low-price products, is how to achieve even incremental growth in a slow-growth environment. Thus, you have two interconnected missions: find new customers to grow your business and keep Wall Street happy.

For brand managers and retailers this conundrum takes on special significance: Now that there is no "average" customer, it stands to reason that consumers aren't stopping at the traditional watering holes. The dynamic of the changing marketplace is what I call "the thinning middle."

WHAT IS THE THINNING MIDDLE?

Traditionally, consumers shopped at one of three types of retailers: luxury stores (e.g., Neiman Marcus or Tiffany), middle-level stores (a department or chain store such as Macy's, Bloomingdale's, or JC Penney), and discounters (e.g., Kmart, Target, Wal-Mart, or Meijer). These categories hold for brands as well: luxury or designer (Ralph Lauren); the middle sector, which could be any national brand (e.g., Levi-Strauss); and the discount sector, which could be private label brands (e.g., Jaclyn Smith).

But with the average income increasing in the United States at a rate of 2.5 percent, according to Hewitt Associates, and the rise in the cost of food in the United States rising an average of 3.5 percent, brands and retailers are finding it difficult to lure the customer into luxury stores. So what are Tiffany and other luxury retailers and brands doing? They're redefining their target consumers by offering more affordable prices that will appeal to a wider range of consumers. Tiffany is a great example of a brand that has established new parameters for its customer base. It moved its strategy from selling products that were no lower than $200 four years ago to selling something that you can get for $60—and with that great Tiffany quality, service, and

Shoppers at all levels want luxury items—but on sale. Low-end consumers are trading up and looking for sales at trendy discounters such as Target, and middle-income customers, who usually shop at department stores, are buying lower-priced luxury brands (e.g., Ralph Lauren Polo).

experience. You can even get that $60 key chain in the sig-
nature blue box with the blue felt bag and white ribbon.
Figs. 5-1 and 5-2 illustrate this changing dynamic.

What happened was that Tiffany realized that if it was
to grow its market, it needed to appeal to consumers at all
economic levels and offer more affordable price points. In
essence, it moved the defining line of luxury down. Add to
this the service and cachet of shopping in a designer store
and you've got a long-term customer. To consumers, whether
it's a gift or a purchase to indulge oneself, the ability to afford

**FIGURE 5-1   The thinning middle trend is shown by comparing the
earlier part a and the later part b.**

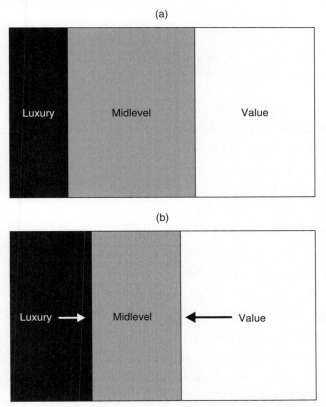

SOURCE: *Beyond the Data with Marshal Cohen.*

FIGURE 5-2 The midlevel fights back. Looking at success at this level
with the right fashion mix and the right messaging.

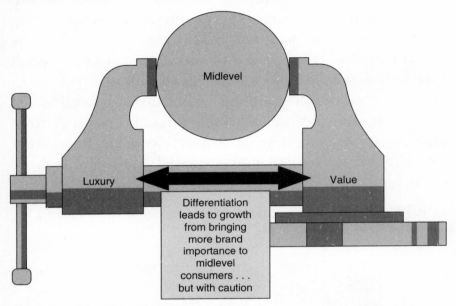

Midlevel

Luxury   Value

Differentiation
leads to growth
from bringing
more brand
importance to
midlevel
consumers . . .
but with caution

SOURCE: *Beyond the Data with Marshal Cohen.*

the original luxury product in its own environment carries a
lot more love than does something from a midlevel, nondescript department store.

Through the process of lowering the opening price
point for luxury, the lines between our traditional three
retail and brand categories have become blurred. What's
happening at the discount level is just as interesting. In an
effort to grow their business, the discount stores, whose
customers are typically hard-pressed for discretionary
spending, have redefined themselves to be upmarket.

Target offers brands such as Mossimo, Cherokee, and
Isaac Mizrahi; Kmart carries Martha Stewart and Joe
Boxer. The discount retailers have introduced more style
and better quality than their standard offerings at only

slightly higher prices. And the brands communicated to customers at all levels that it wasn't only the product's cost that gave it value. The message that you can get more and better for less sank in.

Now consumers at all income levels are comfortable— even proud—that they can find great fashion at incredible prices. Target earned the nickname Tar-gét as if it were a designer store from France. The consumer has responded to these lower-tiered stores favorably and treats them as trendy by the way of reverse chic. I was at a dinner party at the Madison Avenue apartment of an affluent friend. The topic of shopping came up, and the group began sharing stories of how they saved by shopping at warehouse clubs, Target, and Wal-Mart. It was amazing to hear those millionaires proudly admit they actually had walked into a Wal-Mart. When I asked how they were wearing or using the products, it became evident that it was side by side with their expensive products. This has become true across the nation; consumers are pairing designer sweaters with cheap chic jeans for $19.99 and $200 shoes with a blouse that cost $12.99 from H&M and a skirt from a department store that they had from last year.

So, with the low end moving *up* into the midsector and the high end moving *down* into the midsector, you get "the thinning middle." Compounding this phenomenon, in addition to the advent of affordable luxury and the emergence of shabby chic, is the fact that consumers are

---

The Thinning Middle
The low end moves up, and the high end moves down.

shopping differently than they did in the past. They are educating themselves—we hope with your help—on where they can shop to get more value for their money. Having established—either by visiting stores or by doing research in newspapers or magazines or online—where to shop, they are very methodical once they are in their places of purchase. This past holiday season it was fascinating to watch consumers come into stores at the crack of dawn with downloads from the Internet indicating what items were selling at what stores that day with the best prices. They would map out their shopping day strategically. I watched one woman go into a Target to purchase a toaster and a single-serve coffee maker for $4.90 each. Yes, $4.90 each! (The packaging costs almost that much.) Other than those items, she didn't buy anything else, but she bought several of each item. Then she was off to the next store with her list and the keys to the car in hand.

Whether you're a brand manager or a retailer, it is a certainty that you are going be affected by the trend toward a thinning middle. The lower end is able to stay in its sector and trade up, the upper end is able to trade down but remain brand- and store-loyal, and the midsector consumer is being offered less and less by the department store brands. Worse, in their quest for stability and growth, the stores and brands are abandoning their core customers and principles, causing great frustration for those midsector consumers.

What does the brand stand for when it has been selling to a group of core customers for decades and now suddenly targets a whole new consumer base, and what happens to the original customer? Can you imagine shopping at your favorite department store—the one you've been loyal to for years—and finding that the departments you've come to love are gone because the store is going after the teen market? Speakers are blaring, music videos are being broadcast throughout the store, and as you make your way through the chaos, you find a salesperson who is less than helpful. Essentially, the customer has been downsized along with the staff and services of the store. What kind of message does this communicate to the consumer about your brand? By alienating core customers, midsector brands and stores might have increased the number of customers in one demographic but lost their long-term market base. In point of fact, department stores have lost 5 percent of their sales over the last eight years to mass merchants and specialty brands and retailers.

FAUX LUXURY

One of two consumers shopping in department stores today is also shopping in discount stores. A second factor that compounds the challenge to midlevel brands is the fact that brands in general have become so similar in terms of style that consumers would rather buy a knockoff and buy four for the price of one than purchase the authentic item. Taking this a step further, I've have seen products sold by two different types of retailers that are so similar in style that telling the difference between them was nearly impossible. It's what I call the "Sea of Sameness."

Affordable prices make a wider array of products more accessible than ever. In researching the effect of the Sea of Sameness on consumer purchasing, I did a little fieldwork that started with a pair of designer shoes being sold at an upscale department store for $99. According to the sales

> ## The Sea of Sameness is a brand killer!

associate on the floor, that particular item was among the best-selling shoes of the week. I had to go to a second location in the store to purchase those hot-selling shoes and spent 45 minutes on the entire process. My next stop was a Target about one-quarter mile down the road, so close that you could see one store from the other. Once in Target, I walked directly to the shoe department, and right there on the end cap, facing the aisle, was a display of Isaac Mizrahi shoes that were so similar to the best-selling pair I had just purchased at an upscale department store that I couldn't believe it. I purchased them as well; the whole process took 12 minutes, and that included getting into my car so I could go back to the department store and return the first pair!

This example truly reflects the perspective of consumers who know they can get four pairs of shoes from Target for the price of one pair from a department store. They are willing to sacrifice quality, understanding that it's more about disposable fashion, and they don't feel guilty when they ruin the shoes by scuffing them or stepping in a puddle of salty snow five weekends before the Christmas holiday in the mall parking lot. The bottom line is that consumers are making trade-offs. Brand managers need to be keenly aware of what these trade-offs are if they want to reach customers physically as well as through their message.

GET SOME PERSONALITY

With the ailing core consumer, midsector brands and stores are attempting to replace lost revenue by focusing on providing other offerings that create a unique identity for the brand and the retailer and elevate them from the Sea of Sameness, where all merchandise looks and feels alike. To do this, brands at the middle level are going to have to get some personality.

Successful brands grow with their customers and excite them with new features, offering the opportunity to remain loyal by adapting to consumers' standards, demands, and interests as they mature and by refining their brands accordingly. Toyota is a great example of a brand that went from downmarket to midmarket and is now appealing to buyers in the upper market by expanding its product line to include a luxury model (the Lexus) while maintaining its reputation for quality and style and, for the most part, affordability.

Ralph Lauren is a business that found a way to appeal to consumers at all levels. Ralph Lauren first came to prominence with its Polo line, an upper-end brand of apparel. Over time the company has introduced 13 brands that appeal to all levels of consumers: the Purple label for high-end buyers and Chaps for the low end. The brands in between include Polo Sport, Polo Jeans, and Lauren, all of which focus on different lifestyles or segments of the market. You can add to the mix the recent addition of a retail concept focused on the young adult consumer called Rugby with a test store in Boston.

LESS ISN'T ALWAYS MORE

Stores and brands have embarked on a campaign to reduce product offerings in order to cut back on promotion and inventory costs. Although this looks good on paper, I have seen countless examples of production cost-cutting methods that actually cause greater declines in sales. If your brand is looking to attract new customers, this is not the time to decrease product offerings.

A hypothetical: If your brand is thriving in the young adult market and you want to expand to the midsector market by focusing on 35- to 55-year-olds, would you cut back on the models that cater to the 18- to 24-year-olds? Would you just eliminate all the styles or just do away with the underperformers? It is understandable to eliminate some models to make room for new ones, but a balance must be maintained. Volkswagen, for instance, dominated the young adult market with the Jetta. When it wanted to tap into the luxury market and appeal to older customers, it added a high-priced model and introduced the Phaeton, with a manufacturer's suggested retail price of $45,000. The car has a host of top-end features and competes with other upscale models, including Lexus, Mercedes, and BMW. Wisely, Volkswagen didn't abandon its core customer and stop producing or marketing the Jetta. It absorbed the cost of creating a new product and redefining its brand and successfully reached an entirely new customer base.

THE IMPORTANCE OF TIMING

It's important to understand not only how and where customers make their purchases but *when*. Brands and retailers

> Brands and stores that eliminate a product only to reintroduce it when customers clamor to have it back face a sinkhole of costs and the need to devise an entirely new branding effort. Educating and Exploring can help you avoid this type of strategic blunder.

need to shake up their thinking about selling seasons. Our most recent research indicates that consumers really don't want to buy their swimwear in *January*. Only 7 percent of consumers consider themselves leaders when it comes to purchasing behavior. This means that only 7 percent have the desire to be the first on their block to own the newest product, the latest model, or the early fashions. This 7 percent reflects a drop-off from 8 percent just two years ago, and our belief is that it will drop further as consumers continue to try to buy more with less. Is it in the midsector brands' best interest to continue to focus solely on this leading 7 percent? Wouldn't they be better served by offering products on a schedule that is closer to that of their customers?

Timberland has done a great job of shifting its product launch and delivery to be in sync with the purchasing season. Many brands ship all their winter goods in July and August and try to benefit form the longer selling period while waiting for the cold weather to hit. That is not a great idea since the merchandise that the majority of consumers are shopping for in August is meant to be worn then, not in the months ahead. Timberland expanded its product line to include footwear for any season while shipping seasonal footwear when interest was most high. A pair of lined boots would hit the stores in October, not August. While offering a shorter selling season, Timberland saw a healthier sell-through with no need to promote and mark down the lined boots prematurely because they hadn't sold in the dog days of summer.

KEEP DIGGING

To better manage these consumer purchasing trends, take the time to learn what your customers want, when they want it, what type of lifestyle they live, and what their aspirations

> Create a flow of product that connects with consumers by tapping into their timing needs.

are. Create a flow of product that connects with the consumers by matching their needs, desires, and timing. History has a habit of repeating itself; learn to utilize research to analyze and understand historical shifts in behavior and timing. You can't accomplish this simply by studying internal sales information. Brands tend to look at what they sold and when. How will you know how much you can sell outside your sweet spot when you have neither the right product nor the opportunity to assess the impact of alternative timing?

The impact this lack of knowledge has on branding and sales strategies hit me recently during a strategy session with a manufacturer. I asked why the company hadn't sold more plus-sized apparel. Their answer was that they sold a certain amount last year and bought the same amount this year. They were very proud that they did their homework and were prepared to match the sales from last year. I respectfully posed a hypothetical question to the group: If you have 12 pieces of something and 1 in each size, how many could you possibly sell? "Twelve" was the answer I got. That is correct. But what if you had 2 of each size; could you have sold more than 12? Sure, but we sold only 12 last year, and to buy 24 pieces would be too risky. Do you realize that if you sell just one more out of a dozen, you will grow your business by 8 percent instantly? I asked.

Why not learn from outside information what sizes you could try to sell more of? Today that merchant is growing its business by well over 8 percent and watching sales grow in places it never thought they could. History has its place, but don't let it rule you.

6

THE SUPERSIZING
OF AMERICA

THE NEXT TIME YOU'RE AT AN AIRPORT or at the movies, take a good hard look at the people around you. How many overweight people can you count? I know this is not new information, but the number of overweight individuals is growing, and these folks represent a whole new type of customer. Yet the absence of products marketed to the needs of overweight people suggests that businesses are missing a real opportunity to grow their customer base, market share, and revenues (see Fig. 6-1).

THE SCALE DOESN'T LIE

According to the Centers for Disease Control and Prevention, an estimated 30 percent of U.S. adults—over 60 million people—are obese, defined as having a body mass

FIGURE 6-1 Americans appear to be losing interest in "being on any diet." This does not mean that fewer Americans say they are actively dieting.

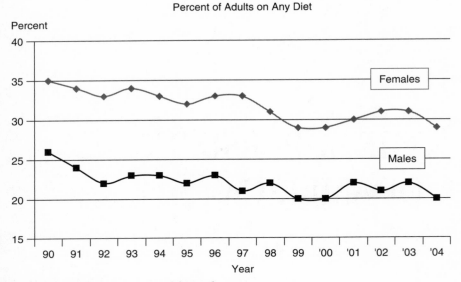

Percent of Adults on Any Diet

SOURCE: NPD Group's HealthTrack service.

index (BMI) of 30 or higher. That means that 3 in 10 Americans are obese. An estimated 65 percent of U.S. adults are overweight, which is defined as having a BMI of 25 or higher. At least one in two Americans is overweight—if it's not you, it's the guy sitting next to you. No matter how you slice it, there are (forgive me) *huge* opportunities to grow your brand or product with this "supersizing" of America issue in mind. Whether your customers want to elevate their lifestyles by losing weight, eating healthier, being more active, dressing more appropriately, or just feeling more comfortable with their supersizes, there is certainly a way for you to take advantage of these opportunities.

Of course the diet industry has been marketing toward weight loss for as long as anyone alive can remember. Americans have been dieting for generations, but what is interesting is that according to NPD Foodworld's Health Track Service, Americans steadily have been decreasing their participation in formal diets. Yes, Americans are participating actively in diets less and less. Since 1985 the percentage of women who state that they are on a diet has dropped from 35 percent to 29 percent. It has been almost a steady decline for the last 20 years. Men likewise have decreased their likeliness to diet even when they clearly need to. Men stated in 1985 that 26 percent of them were on a diet, and that has decreased to 20 percent currently.

Dieting has proved to be an interesting business opportunity. It is more about diet trends than it is about new diets. You may think that the diets on the market today are new, but the Atkins diet, for instance, has been around for over 30 years. The Atkins diet recently caught the attention of repeat dieters as well as the newly rotund. According to NPD Foodworld, it has become the top diet adults are aware of and the third most popular diet adults have ever tried (see Fig. 6-2).

FIGURE 6-2   The diet of choice is the one you make up. The top diet tried by Americans is the one described as "my own diet."

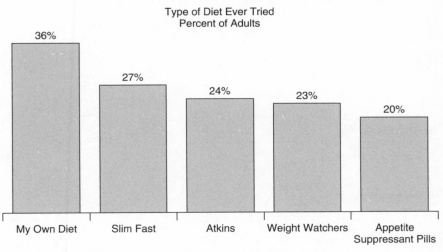

SOURCE: NPD Group's Dieting Monitor, average for 2004.

Even with all the marketing done for diet plans, all the books, and all the news about the success of this diet or that, Americans' favorite diet plan is the one they make up for themselves. According to the data collected from consumers directly in the NPD Group's Dieting Monitor, Americans, when asked, stated that when they tried a diet, 36 percent chose their own diet plan.

With all this attention, knowledge, and even product available to make dieting something a bit easier to associate with, why are fewer Americans dieting? An NPD Foodworld study (see Fig. 6-3) showed that when asked how much they agree or disagree with the statement "I would like to lose at least 20 pounds," over 61 percent of Americans age 17 and up stated that they would. Between agree, somewhat agree, mostly agree, and definitely agree, Americans know they need to lose weight. But what are they willing to do to lose that weight? Could it be that incremental changes in lifestyle are the answer—and an opportunity?

FIGURE 6-3   It is true that most of us would like to lose weight. But note the number of people who disagree with this statement. It is similar to the number of people who have never been on a diet.

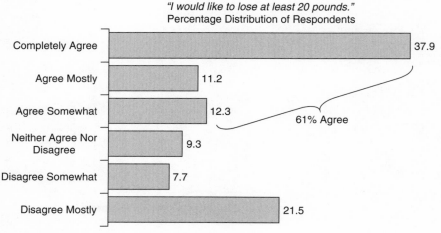

SOURCE: NPD Group's Nutritional Tracking.

Somewhere between the types of foods Americans eat and an increasingly sedentary lifestyle centered on television and video games, the American consumer has, on the whole, gotten bigger. The number of hours the average American watches television in a week has increased since television was introduced in the 1950s, as has the number of processed foods consumed and the offerings of leisure activities that require no more physical activity than wiggling a thumb and staring at a screen. (Fig. 6-4 cites a few factors that have prompted consumers to practice unhealthy lifestyles.) Go ahead, open up a bag of chips and let's talk about this.

With the exception of the food industry, which is using technology to create low-carb and fat-free options (often

FIGURE 6-4   What prompted you to practice an unhealthy lifestyle? The frequency of three responses are shown, for males and females. All respondents can use help learning how to be more healthy, and maybe they won't be so tired.

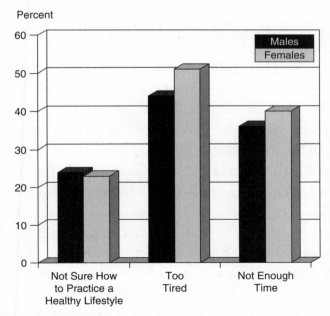

SOURCE: NPD Health/Lifestyle Poll.

sold alongside the original fully caloric items), the chance to engage this growing (I promise, that's the last time) market has slipped by. With just the gentlest nudge you probably could get the average overweight American consumer to make a move in the right direction—get more active, lose some weight already—or buy a product or service that very gracefully caters to his or her robust size. Leisure activities represent an opportunity, as do clothes that fit better, cars that fit better, and any number of seats in public arenas such as movie theaters, airliners, and anywhere else an overweight consumer needs to fit. And remember, more than half of us are overweight. Again, forgive me, but this is a *huge* market! Somewhere between the notion that losing weight would elevate a lifestyle and the idea that a better fit would feel good is a business opportunity you probably never have thought about. Start thinking!

REACHING THE LARGER CONSUMER

Here's a thought: About 10 percent of the population is left-handed. There are scissors, sports equipment, can openers, and even cars designed for southpaws, and they make up only some 10 percent of the population. Well, 65 percent of us are overweight, but how many products are designed for this market? Not many. Maybe lefties are less sensitive about being called left-handed than overweight people are about being called, well, fat. But there's gold in them thar waistlines if only we gave it a little thought.

I'm reminded of the supersizing of America with almost every step I take. I was on a flight to Florida that was being delayed at the gate. I had given a presentation in New York earlier that day and had no room for tardiness in getting to

Miami to give another presentation later that day. After twenty minutes passed, I asked the gate agent why we were being delayed and was told that they were in need of six additional seat belt extenders as the plane had only four on board and that was not enough. I asked the gate agent if four was the normal amount, and he informed me that it was but that this was becoming an increasing problem. With that in mind, I started to notice just how many people on flights were extremely overweight. There were quite a few. I also began to wonder: If we are all getting bigger, why are the seats and legroom getting smaller? American Airlines just a short time ago tried to introduce increased legroom in coach, but economic factors made it impossible. Still, they tried. When you consider that one of the biggest travel complaints is lack of room and then consider that as a whole we're all getting bigger, it's no wonder we complain.

Movie theaters are starting to pay close attention to elevating the viewing experience as well as the comfort factor. Recently renovated theaters and certainly most of the new ones feature wider aisles and more legroom as well as bigger, more comfortable seats. Cup holders and snack trays also help make it more comfortable and enticing to purchase items at the concession stand, which is where much of a theater's money is made. Some theaters even have concession carts come into the aisles so that patrons don't even have to get up out of their seats. Theater chains explored, evaluated, and elevated, and it has paid off for them.

The auto industry has confronted the ever-increasing need for space of Americans. SUVs aren't popular because they can be driven off-road: Statistics show that only 20 percent of all SUVs sold are ever driven off-road. Part of the allure of the larger vehicles—SUVs, vans, and larger sedans—is the increased passenger room. Automakers are even starting to market the ease of entering and exiting the vehicle by offering what they call "captain seats" that swivel to give the passengers more space and an easier time getting into and out of the vehicle. The positioning of some of the instruments and displays is being moved around in the cabin to make it easier for the size-challenged to be able to view and manipulate the controls. There are so many areas that have just begun to scratch the surface of catering to larger consumers, and the numbers prove that there are more and more of them every day.

Let's explore one area that has done very little in the way of marketing to the larger consumer: the fashion industry. In 1985 the most popular dress size for women was a size 8. That means that more women purchased clothes in a size 8 than in any other size. In 2004 the most popular size was a size *14*. Although some people argue that designers and retailers are making the product bigger to keep the egos of their consumers feeling good—I call it vanity sizing—that wouldn't account for the almost doubling of sizes. Sure, some clothing makers arguably are making the product bigger, but there are some that are making the sizes smaller. With so many of the brands and retailers focused on teens and young adults, they are making the product smaller and tighter to the body.

In a recent NPD study of 21,000 women, over 40 percent of them stated that they have purchased a plus-size product for themselves. The study also revealed that consumers often wear different sizes on the top and on the bottom. Some even shop for their wardrobe needs in plus-size departments or stores for their tops and in regular-size departments and shops for their bottoms. The equation is also just as likely to occur the opposite way: plus size on the bottom and regular on the top. Why is it that if 40 percent of women purchase a plus size, plus sizes account for only

18 percent of the dollar sales in the United States? And why is it that women (and men, for that matter) need to shop in two different places and sometimes floors or stores to complete one outfit?

One of the biggest complaints by consumers about plus sizes and big and tall sizes is that they don't have the choice of product that the regular-size business offers. Is this true? You bet it is. Take one look at the offerings in these areas in the department stores. Some stores are doing a better job at it lately, but they still have a long way to go. Many designers just got into the business of offering a plus size or a big and tall collection.

I recall speaking with one designer from Calvin Klein Couture, the highest-end division of that company's apparel business. When I asked why they don't carry anything over a size 12 in their store, he responded by saying, "I don't want to ruin the image of our brand with people who are larger-sized wearing the clothes that the women who work hard at staying fit and trim would wear." I asked about the shortsightedness of that statement, and he said they would rather lose the volume than the image. I am happy to say that today Calvin Klein does offer large-size clothes, but it was only recently that the designer market started to address this issue and offer collections to the plus-size market. This really came about through pressure from the retailers as one of the fastest growing segments in fashion happened to be plus sizes and became too important to ignore.

NICHE SEGMEMENTATION

Beyond offering more plus and large sizes, what can be done to reach this segment of customers? In the next chapter we'll discuss segmenting consumers by lifestyle versus age, but here we'll address niche segmentation. Any multidimensional strategy should include not only offering more products but also offering different product. Not every plus-size consumer is a regular length either. Plus petite may sound like an oxymoron, but there is a group of consumers who are plus size in width and short in length. According to the data collected by NPD, they represent 8 percent of the women's market by need, not by sales. Kmart does a great job at marketing to these women, but few other stores do. The other areas for niche markets in the women's plus-size market are plus tall and plus junior sizes, also two very underserved markets.

The challenge here has been that until recently very few retailers were willing to hear me cry out about the opportunity in these niche markets. The focus for growth understandably has been on looking for numbers that would offer at least 5 percent growth, but with apparel sales declining consistently from 2000 to 2003, the retailers needed to find any kind of growth at all. Size niches represented an opportunity they needed to explore.

How big can this business become? Don't laugh, but at this rate the fastest growing segments for apparel will continue to include the plus-size and big and tall businesses. Americans are showing no signs of getting smaller. Diets remain the primary form of weight loss, and dieters still account for a significantly smaller proportion of the population than is needed. Also keep in mind that we will need to watch what happens as the baby boomers age beyond the capacity to act younger than their age. Although we may be nearing the time when the boomers will start taxing the social security system, we also are going to reach a point where the boomers who are turning 60 and eventually 70 may not be bungee jumping as often and just might have changing needs in sizes for apparel as well.

Footwear is another example of the growing consumer. Are you aware that the three most popular sizes for women's fashion footwear went from 8, 7, and 7½ in 1985 to 8, 9, and 8½ in 2004? Although this doesn't seem like a significant difference, it surely is. Retailers generally purchase only one size 9 for every 12 pairs of shoes they buy of a style, yet it amazes vendors to learn that generally if they buy one size of a style, they will be able to sell only one pair.

When I ask many retailers why they don't buy more size 9s, the second most popular size, they inform me that history dictates that they sell only one pair. That makes sense since if they buy only one, the likelihood of selling only one is pretty great. When I then ask why not try to sell a second pair, I hear the inevitable answer that they buy only what they sell. I could scream! How out of touch with the consumer can you be? Don't make the historical mistake of thinking that what once sold will continue to sell. Don't make the mistake of thinking that things don't change much. They do. Use research, both in the field and from analysts, to raise your awareness of the dynamics shaping your market.

WHAT THIS MEANS FOR YOU

The lesson here is simple: We need to look at each and every business to determine whether the needs of the changing consumer are being met. Are we offering products that are dealing with the size and age issue? Not all things remain the same, and the consumer is a living, breathing, and ever-changing entity. Sometimes it is as simple as asking consumers what they care about. In a recent NPD poll consumers identified their priorities for interests and desires, stating that women are most interested in health and fitness, followed by electronics/computers, whereas men named electronics/computers number one and health and fitness number two.

How is it possible that today, with health and fitness being the number one and number two interests for women and men, respectively, consumers state that they just don't know how to live a healthier lifestyle? In a recent consumer poll of over 31,000 people, more than 20 percent of the women and men stated they don't know how to participate in a healthier lifestyle. The number one answer was that they were too tired. So how does this help you? By being a lifestyle brand and educating consumers that you understand their need to live a healthier life, your brand can help them learn more about living it, practicing it, and even buying it. Explore ways to educate consumers on what they need to learn. Whether you are selling athletic shoes, tablecloths, or electronics, it doesn't matter.

You have the ability to communicate to consumers that yours is a brand that belongs in their lives. Your brand is about making their life better; it is not just a product they should buy. Create a relationship with the consumers to help them. Whether on your website or in ad campaigns, hang tags, product information, or even follow-up programs such as newsletters and e-mails that target key interests, your brand has the opportunity to connect in a way that will create powerful word of mouth and lead to brand growth. It is as simple as creating a path to allow the consumer to sign up for participation in a program that you can run in house or farm out and feature other companies looking to partner with you. Answer questions such as how to make your clothes last longer and how to choose the right computer system. Offer ways to learn what is the right form of exercise or diet based on information from bona fide experts. Help people learn how to participate in causes they might care about.

The opportunity we find in the supersizing of America is one of lifestyle elevation, along with exploring, educating, and evaluating. All Five E's apply here and to all other areas of consumer interest. What is the right electronic gadget to buy to make their lives simpler? What will this item do for consumers that will be helpful, or will the learning curve intimidate them and make this yet another electronic item that sits in the box and does not get used? Consumers need to be educated, and they *want* to be educated. Learn what the opportunities are to grow your brand and business by addressing their needs. They will thank you for it in many ways.

7

DID YOU JUST CALL ME MA'AM?

IT'S ALL ABOUT LIFESTYLE, NOT AGE

If you are still using age to define your target consumer, you had better rethink your approach. Consumers are not interested in having age dictate their pursuits or purchase decisions, and they're not attracted to brands that do that. Whether they are actively living a certain lifestyle or aspiring to, consumers are seeking out brands and products that support their choices—brands that, like them, look at *how* they live, not *how long* they've lived.

There are countless products and brands across industries that are exploring the wants and desires of the 30-plus crowd, elevating their own messages and offerings to meet that market's lifestyle requirements and concerns. Beauty products with sunblock, athletic shoes designed for the

> Consumers no longer are defined by their age but by the type of life they lead.

urban dweller, SUVs created for the adventuring family of four, and the like, are all building their brand identities and messages on the lifestyle choices of their customers. Don't focus on the age of your customer; look at what you can do to create products and services that correlate with lifestyle choices. (Age as a secondary factor—see Fig. 7-1.)

LIFESTYLE BRANDING

Department stores and midlevel brands have been so focused on getting close to younger consumers that they've

FIGURE 7-1   Adult spending on apparel by age. Dollar sales in the 12 months ending January 2003.

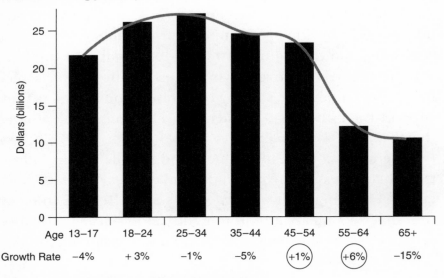

SOURCE: NPD Fashionworld Consumer Data.

The Shrinking Generation Gap

Today consumers of all ages are using similar products, listening to the same music, and even sharing in purchase decisions. Learn what causes this, find out why marketing your brand is different because of this, and see just how small the gap between generations has become. Brands and products are created to address lifestyle choices, not the perceived needs of consumers of a certain age (see Fig. 7-2).

lost their identity and appeal among core customers. Fueling this trend is the realization that teens are making many of their own purchasing decisions as well as affecting those of the family and have more money to spend than did their counterparts in past generations. However, the great attention brands and stores have paid to this segment has resulted in shifts across the board, from how product is sized to

FIGURE 7-2 Consumers of all ages are sharing these interests.

- Music
  - U2, Beatles, Rock, R&B
  - Cover Songs (Shaggy: "Angel")
- Movies
  - Kids' Movies with Adult Humor
  - Remake (Retro) Films
    - *Jetsons, Brady Bunch, Dennis the Menace, Scoobie Doo, Spiderman*
- Sports
- Activities
- Purchase Decisions
  - Who decides which model to pick for the family car?
- Product Advancement
  - Who helps Mom and Dad learn which digital camera to buy?
- Wardrobe sharing

SOURCE: NPD Group.

where it is sold to an entire redefinition of the brand message. Some brands and stores have made their products so trendy and skimpy that anyone over the age of seven would have to be poured into those products. Although I say this partly in jest, I do mean it. Several retailers and even brands have decided that for them to remain true teen brands, they need to downsize their fit. Department stores as a group went to such extremes that they lost market share and dollar sales to the tune of almost double-digit declines. They tried to adjust their approach so that other age markets were included, but by then their brand images and messages had gone so far off track that it was almost impossible to lure back core customers.

One strategy that was used to win back the frustrated adult consumer and perhaps redefine a brand's identity was the celebrity spokesperson. How did that work out? Let's look at who actually is spending money on fashion items.

In 2002 teen spending was up over 10 percent for fashion, and it was another 8 percent in 2003, but as I warned my clients, the pendulum was shifting (see Fig. 7-3). Teens were growing less interested in fashion and were gaining interests across a wider range of image-related products. Cell phones became more important than the right pair of jeans. MP3 players became the item that kids would negotiate with their parents to buy for them if they shifted from spending $80 on jeans from Abercrombie and started to shop at the more realistically priced American Eagle or even Target. That negotiation worked as it seemed that this new crop of teens was the first in decades to have been put on a budget. Thus, this steadfast focus on the younger consumer worked—for about a nanosecond.

Teen spending shifted from fashion to personal electronics. When one adds to this the fact that teens revolve out of their age bracket in a very short four years, it becomes clear

FIGURE 7-3   Apparel age and category highlights. Dollar sales, February–July 2004.

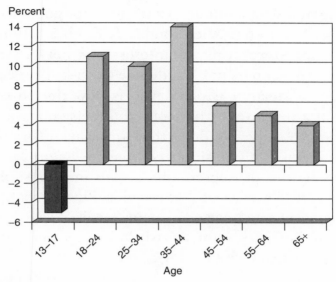

SOURCE: NPD Group.

that brands need to reintroduce themselves continuously to grab the next crop of teens. If you market to a single specific age segment to the exclusion of others and establish your brand only in that consumer segment, you are facing some significant limitations. If your brand or product currently defines itself and creates its image according to age, you need to start all over with the Five E's to determine if you are tapping into lifestyle needs, not just behaviors that seem to be dictated by age.

I FEEL YOUR PAIN

Despite the allure of teen spending, businesses cannot ignore the adult consumer, who wields the highest spending power overall. It pains me to learn that the first impulse of some brands is to ignore their loyal customers merely because those customers have grown beyond the age of their targeted demographic. That's just not good business. On a field trip to one Abercrombie & Fitch location I was told that the store's primary interest was not in targeting consumers beyond its main audience of 18- to 24-year-olds. Try telling a steady customer who is now the 28-year-old mother of a 6-year-old who looks and feels young and certainly feels that she can dress that way that the brand is no longer for her. This position completely ignored the fact that one-quarter of Abercrombie's consumer base is older than the target market of 24-year-olds. Does it make sense to throw away one-quarter of your earnings? No. So why would any business want to risk losing 25 percent of its potential revenue (see Fig. 7-4)?

FIGURE 7-4   Apparel spending by age for 2003 and 2004.

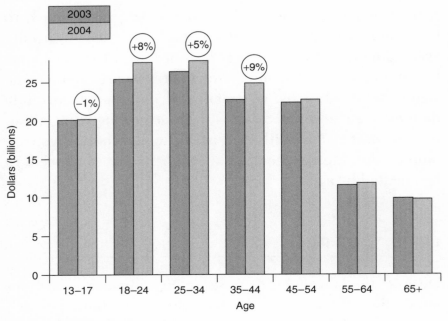

SOURCE: NPD Fashionworld.

I am seeing this attitude changing among luxury and designer brands; in fact, I learned that Abercrombie has announced plans to open a store whose target market will be 25- to 35-year-olds. That represents some improvement, but I worry that it's just not enough. And then you have to wonder if the brand actually knows enough about its older customers to reach them effectively. They should take a lesson from Liz Claiborne, which is an excellent example of a business that continues to appeal to a core demographic but has expanded its brand image and product line to grow with the age and lifestyle changes of its "maturing" customers.

Back in the 1980s Liz Claiborne was a product designed for the young adult career-oriented woman and was the creator of what now is known as the "career" department in stores today. Some specialty chains have grown out of this concept, but Liz Claiborne has remained true to its core customer. As the consumer aged, so did the focus of the Liz Claiborne product, but the company also continued to keep its eye on the next wave of young adults. Instead of reinventing itself every few years for a new crop of young career upstarts, Liz Claiborne kept designing clothes and accessories for its customers as they entered other phases of their lives. The company maintained its loyal customer base and at the same time achieved growth by appealing to younger consumers. Liz Claiborne also did a great job of getting the junior career woman to think about its products when it came time to build a professional wardrobe. I recall watching ad after ad come out with the Liz models looking more and more like the company's ever-changing consumers. Just because a woman turned 50, that didn't mean she had to turn in her wardrobe and start wearing house dresses. Liz Claiborne offered outfits for women who wanted to age gracefully—or not at all.

TABLE 7-1   Traditional and Lifestyle Consumers

Traditional (Demographic)	Lifestyle (Psychographic)
Individual	Community
Consumer	Copurchaser
Market segment	Market integration
Offering	Exploring
Corporation	Cooperation
Brand image	Brand community
Transaction	Transformation
Destination	Journey
Sell	Educate

Many businesses have the right intention of appealing to the over-30 consumer. I have been advising clients for several years now not to lose sight of this very powerful, affluent, and spend-happy market. However, brands often remain too heavily focused on the younger generation, partially for the sake of image and also in the belief that the younger generation *traditionally* spends more money on fashion, music, and electronics. Later in this chapter we'll look at who the real spenders are across these industries.

Table 7-1 highlights the differences between generations and shows how the consumers who have the buying power view themselves.

COMPANIES THAT GET IT

Honda is an example of a company completely missing its target consumer. The Honda Element, a hybrid between a sport-utility vehicle and a van, has been on the road for a few years now. This vehicle, in my opinion, is one of the ugliest cars on the road. No offense to those of you who own one; I am sure it is a very reliable and functional vehicle. I just don't get the design and those black trim highlights. But that is not the issue here. This car was designed to offer young drivers, targeted as 25-year-old active consumers, the opportunity to drive a vehicle that had them in mind.

When the model was introduced to the consumer, it was done with an attempt to demonstrate the Element's ability to deliver a car that was created particularly with the young adult in mind, and the brand directly correlated age with extracurricular pursuits. One commercial featured two people bungee jumping off a cliff alongside their Honda Element. The second commercial depicted a couple mountain biking down a muddy trail, driving their bikes right up to their Honda Element. They even were shown rolling their muddy bikes right into the rear bed of the vehicle with bike rails set up for transporting their bikes without any hassle or outside stowing. The third commercial showed three surfers living the surfer lifestyle out of the Honda Element on the beach and loving life. This was all about selling the car to a younger generation that was perceived as having the most active, fun lifestyles bar none. Honda even produced one of the optional models to boast a "kick ass stereo system" offering an incredible sound experience with no need to upgrade on your own that included the ultimate in audio: a Bose speaker system.

What Honda didn't expect was that the consumers who were going to respond to this product were not the targeted 25-year-olds but the 45-plus-year-olds. How could this be? How could the commercials, the car's design, and the focus be so far off? advertisers and automakers wanted to know. Between style, price, and its overall lack of appeal to the first-time car buyer, Honda missed the 18- to 24-year-old audience it originally had targeted but did reach the older consumer. In an April 2004 article *Car and Driver* magazine confirmed this trend (http://www.caranddriver.com/article.asp?section_id=17&article_id=7881&page_number=1) and had its staff members run their own tests on the vehicle. The car got good reviews for its ruggedness, price, and performance, but the style factor just wasn't there. Clearly, for the first-time car buyer, style was part of the value equation.

Honda and, more important, the advertising agencies forgot one important thing: Just because people turn 45, that doesn't mean they stop living and loving life. Consumers at 45 years old and beyond are getting to the point in their lives where they can focus on living the lifestyle they have always aspired to but had to put on hold to raise a family or develop a career. If Honda's intent was to sell solely to the younger market or the first-time car buyer . . . surprise, the majority of customers were over 40.

The cruise line industry has figured it out, but that industry did so in a similar fashion. While it was looking for growth and focusing on targeting the younger consumer, adventure cruises were born. But not all adventure cruises are filled with 25-year-olds seeking whale watching and jet skiing alongside a glacier. Forty-five-year-olds are taking these trips as well. One of the fastest growing segments in the travel business is adventure trips for the 45-plus market.

Does taking a cruise in the Caribbean and dining and sunbathing to your heart's content sound appealing? Maybe taking a few hours off the boat to visit an island to shop at the open-air market for some souvenirs does it for some vacation seekers, but the increase in spending on adventure vacations means that consumers are leaning toward going on a cruise in the waters of Alaska, jet skiing, hang gliding, and even playing miniature golf with friends to the sound of the horn disrupting the big putt, as in the commercial for Norwegian Cruise Lines. They figured it out. It is lifestyle and adventure they are selling; it is not about age segments.

The makers of Volvo got it too. Will buying a car that offers a ventilation system that lets you change the air filter in your car shift your brand loyalty? Well, if you are a consumer who wants to live in the healthiest environment possible, this is the car for you. Whether it is food, cars, homes, clothing, or electronics, almost anything today can be viewed with the lifestyle concept in mind. It is not only about a healthy lifestyle either.

Learning what is important to a consumer in purchase decision making can make all the difference in terms of someone buying your brand rather than another. If you know that price and health are the top two influencers for purchase decisions, emphasizing them in your design and packaging is critical. Sometimes you may not win the price wars and be able to offer the lowest-price product, but as we discussed earlier, sometimes consumers are willing to pay more if they know they will get more. It is up to you to educate them on those benefits and touch points.

A WORD ABOUT LIFE STAGES

Although lifestyle choices and aspirations are the primary drivers of purchasing behavior, *life stages* are an important secondary force. Now, keep in mind that I said life *stage*, not *age*, although the two at times overlap.

In terms of the types of products bought and the shopping experience itself, parenthood is arguably the most influential life stage when it comes to shaping consumer purchasing behavior. Families of consumers shop as a unit, meaning that many mothers and daughters are sharing

> Age is no longer the defining line for a brand's identity.
> Consumers will continue to pursue their interests and
> desires well into their continuing life stages.

wardrobes when size permits. Family purchases such as
home entertainment systems and even the family car are
being decided on as a group and in many cases heavily
influenced by younger members of the family.

Music and other forms of entertainment have shifted to
be more inclusive of multiple generations as well. Sampling has become a familiar trend in popular music and
serves multiple purposes: The new song immediately benefits from the best-seller status and nostalgia of the song it
is sampling (remember Shaggy's "Angel"?), and the label
understands that the teens most likely are getting the
money to buy the new CD from their parents, with whom
the sampled song will resonate. Toys and movies are following this trend as well. Hello Kitty, a hot brand in the toy
market, has been resurrected with great success because of
mothers' comfort with the brand. Cabbage Patch and My
Little Pony also have resurfaced. *Shrek* and *Shrek* 2 are
recent examples of movies that seemed to have universal
age appeal, and the tremendous box office revenue of both
movies bears out the wisdom of this approach.

Just take a look at the box office winners for 2004 and
2005 in Table 7-2. In 2004, 5 of the year's top 25 revenue
winners were targeted at viewers of all age groups, yielding
$1,443,772,895 in box office sales. And in 2005 the pat-
tern repeated itself, with 6 of the top 25 movies intended
for both the youth and adult markets, resulting in
$699,769,475 in box office receipts as of this writing.

TABLE 7-2   Top 25 Films at Box Office for 2004 and 2005

2004			
Rank	Film Title	Studio	Gross
1	Shrek 2	DreamWorks	$441,226,247
2	Spider-Man 2	Sony	$373,585,825
3	The Passion of the Christ	Newmarket	$370,274,604
4	Meet the Fockers	Universal	$277,206,540
5	The Incredibles	Buena Vista	$261,044,492
6	Harry Potter and the Prisoner of Azkaban	Warner Bros.	$249,541,069
7	The Day after Tomorrow	Fox	$186,740,799
8	The Bourne Supremacy	Universal	$176,241,941
9	National Treasure	Buena Vista	$170,642,906
10	The Polar Express	Warner Bros.	$162,775,358
11	Shark Tale	DreamWorks	$160,861,908
12	I, Robot	Fox	$144,801,023
13	Troy	Warner Bros.	$133,378,256
14	Ocean's 12	Warner Bros.	$125,537,276
15	50 First Dates	Sony	$120,908,074
16	Van Helsing	Universal	$120,177,084
17	Fahrenheit 911	Lions Gate	$119,194,771
18	Lemony Snicket's A Series of Unfortunate Events	Paramount	$118,375,262
19	Dodgeball: A True Underdog Story	Fox	$114,326,736
20	The Village	Buena Vista	$114,197,520
21	The Grudge	Sony	$110,359,362
22	Collateral	DreamWorks	$101,005,703
23	The Aviator	Miramax	$100,444,305
24	The Princess Diaries 2: Royal Engagement	Buena Vista	$95,170,481
25	Million Dollar Baby	Warner Bros.	$90,726,186

TABLE 7-2 *(Contd.)*

	2005		
Rank	**Film Title**	**Studio**	**Gross**
1	*Star Wars: Episode III—Revenge of the Sith*	Fox	$271,193,000
2	*Hitch*	Sony	$177,575,142
3	*Robots*	Fox	$126,288,325
4	*The Pacifier*	Buena Vista	$110,341,629
5	*Are We There Yet?*	Sony	$82,301,521
6	*The Ring Two*	DreamWorks	$76,074,616
7	*Constantine*	Warner Bros.	$75,526,444
8	*Sin City*	Dimension	$73,433,000
9	*The Interpreter*	Universal	$69,233,000
10	*Guess Who*	Sony	$67,962,333
11	*Coach Carter*	Paramount	$67,264,877
12	*Sahara*	Paramount	$66,368,000
13	*The Amityville Horror*	MGM	$64,538,396
14	*Madagascar*	DreamWorks	$61,000,000
15	*Monster-in-Law*	New Line	$60,730,000
16	*The Longest Yard*	Paramount	$60,000,000
17	*White Noise*	Universal	$56,386,759
18	*Be Cool*	MGM	$56,046,979
19	*Hide and Seek*	Fox	$51,100,486
20	*Diary of a Mad Black Woman*	Lions Gate	$50,633,099
21	*Racing Stripes*	Warner Bros.	$49,194,660
22	*The Hitchhiker's Guide to the Galaxy*	Buena Vista	$48,645,000
23	*Miss Congeniality 2: Armed and Fabulous*	Warner Bros.	$47,340,711
24	*Boogeyman*	Sony/Screen Gems	$46,476,484
25	*Kingdom of Heaven*	Fox	$44,974,000

SOURCE: www.movies.com.

What makes adding life stage considerations to your branding message tricky is that you still have to consider age factors since life stages often correlate with specific age categories. To bring the practical needs of age into your lifestyle and life stage brand, design your product or service knowing that there may be particular physical attributes of the aging though active consumer that require some consideration, whether it's balancing fit with style, adding enhancers to beauty products, or making letters and numbers big enough to read. And make sure that these value-added features and the consideration that went into them are reflected in your brand's message.

CREATING A LIFESTYLE BRAND

Don't just look at the age of your consumers; look at how to grow your brand by tapping into their lifestyles. Don't speak just one language, communicate one message, and display one focus; explore ways to utilize a multitier approach to marketing your brands. Look at Ralph Lauren again; that brand transcends all ages. It is about a lifestyle, an aspiration, and an image. Their ads don't feature only one specific age segment. Those ads have a story to tell. One assignment I use in my workshop sessions is to have the participants pull out ads from magazines and choose one that tells a story. I ask the team to create the story from that ad and show how it relates back to the product. It is amazing to hear the results and to see from one photograph how the essence of the brand materializes and how the lifestyle of the consumer and story behind the people or products emerge. But it is even more amazing to see the same ads crop up over and over again.

Moving away from marketing by age segment doesn't mean not focusing on age and life stage, but it does mean learning to get growth from a wider sector of ages. Sometimes it is as simple as getting your consumer base to shift from 45- to 65-year-olds to 40- to 70-year-olds. Although the change in numbers doesn't seem like a lot, I would venture to say that you would appreciate being able to appeal to an additional 2.5 million consumers just by adding an additional year segment to your product. The Five E's are the tools you will use to learn how to become a true lifestyle brand because they allow you tap into the psychology of your customer.

8

THE FIVE E'S
OF MARKETING

W HAT HAPPENS WHEN we become accustomed to seeing something that otherwise might be considered out of place? We don't see it anymore for what it is—a mess. The desk in someone's office is a good example. We may have piles or items scattered about, but we grow unaware of them, and it may even look organized to us; to someone else it might appear to be extremely out of the ordinary.

The point here is that even though to you it looks right, to someone else, in this case the consumer, the message or the product may appear to be out of place or may not be communicating important product features. Sometimes it's as simple as the packaging. Something that you think is obvious is not. Consumers look at one segment of the item—usually the package—and brand owners look at others. As we proceed through this chapter, think of how you or your team is not necessarily the best placed to judge your product.

I tell my clients that they need to get three perspectives: theirs, their team's, and the consumer's. It is not enough to ask those around you. Many product decisions are based on instinct, personal opinion, seat-of-the-pants reactions, or taste level. This is not the way to develop product and marketing programs that work. I find that the best technique is to go out to stores, malls, auto dealers, and other places where your consumers are and ask them directly. They have no mission other than to tell you what they think, and that is a very powerful tool. Or you could hire someone to do it for you. But make sure that the people you hire are not in a sterilized environment, standing there with a clipboard and host of irrelevant questions. Pure research comes from conversations as well as observations that can be done even before a product is finalized, from packaging to actual product. But you have to ask the right questions to elicit valuable consumer opinion.

The NPD Group's approach to crafting consumer surveys is a bit counterintuitive, including questions about what the consumer chooses *not* to buy and where *not* to shop. With most stores collecting sales information on items that actually have sold, it's easy to get weighed down with data on those sales. But what gets lost is the basic question of why something sold or didn't sell. Was it the packaging, the price, the fit? There are a multitude of unanswered questions that need to be explored. Learning how to use research to understand what influences consumer behavior is critical. Use your research, whether it consists of surveys or in-the-field interviews, to learn to think the way consumers think. Evaluate what they think, walk in their shoes, try on their pants, or just shop as they would.

It also is important to get a unbiased perspective as well as an uneducated perspective. Responses that are unbiased have no agenda; they don't come from an individual who works for you or feels that there may be consequences if the answer is not what you want to hear. Fear and comfort don't enter into an unbiased response. "Honey, do I look fat in this dress?" Now get an honest answer to that question.

Uneducated perspectives come from people who have no idea what you are asking them. For example, show a tube of toothpaste that offers a new ingredient to prevent tooth decay to someone who has no idea what it is and relies on the packaging to learn about it, not to someone who is already familiar with it, such as an ad agency employee, staff member, or family member. They already know what the new ingredient does and may not be the best to judges of whether it is being communicated to the uneducated person who ultimately will be the target consumer. Uneducated responses are critical to your research because as consumers, we create an opinion or impression of a product in that fraction of a second I spoke of earlier.

Keep in mind that it's not only awareness that matters: Consumer reaction and associations are important here too. It is these associations that ultimately lead to purchases or referrals. In the apparel market the second most influential factor in buying clothing is word of mouth. The only purchase influencer more powerful than word of mouth for fashion is magazine advertising, which includes advertorials. Advertorials are becoming more and more powerful as consumers feel that if they read or hear about a product through the media in a noncommercial form, there is truth in the reporting. Editorials are first when it comes to influence, but the message takes longer to register as the customer needs to spend the time reading.

Therefore, this doesn't create the instant and often almost guaranteed viewing that an advertisement does. Most ads are viewed but not retained. We are subject to some 3,000 forms of advertising a day, and only 50 percent of those ads are retained even subconsciously; only 1 to 2 percent make it to the conscious portion of our minds. Television advertising plays an important role in shaping purchasing decisions as well.

When you look at how consumers are influenced, it is critical to understand that advertising plays a key role. However, the power of word of mouth, blogging, and other forms of peer influence cannot be ignored.

By utilizing the Five E's you can chart a strategy to get at the aspects of your brand that are important to consumers. You will create a path to learning what is expected of your brand and product and ways to deliver on those expectations. The Five E's can be used to build a better product, market more effectively, and communicate your message more clearly so that it can be translated for you by others. The Five E's of marketing are five activities that, when performed sequentially, will improve *any* marketing effort for any product, brand, or service (see Fig. 8-1). Let's look at each one individually and see how it works. We'll also consider all the E's throughout the rest of the book so that you can see how to use them and make them part of your marketing effort.

EDUCATE

The education link is internal, external, and direct to the consumer. By internal, I mean you and your team. By external, I mean your distributors and retailers and anyone else who comes between your product and the consumer.

FIGURE 8-1   Here are the five E's by which to thrive.

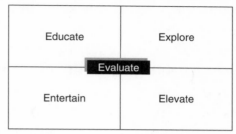

SOURCE: NPD Group.

First, find ways to make sure your team is aware of your company: what it does, what it stands for, and, most important, what the mission is for the year. You can't accomplish your company's mission fully if you don't know what it is. It sounds simple and elementary, but I cannot tell you how many times I meet with companies that don't communicate the core message and focus of the company or communicate what the parent company does.

I was recently in a meeting with a client that licenses a popular brand of shoes. I happened to ask about the parent company and how it was dealing with learning and incorporating the heritage of the parent company. Nobody knew! They had no idea what the parent company's core business was. They knew they had a hot property—the shoes were selling—but they had almost no interaction with anyone on what the parent company was all about.

Why is this so shocking to me? How can a brand allow someone to license out its name and not have the essence of the brand communicated to the designers, the production team, the sellers, and the marketers? Now think about the message as it gets communicated to the consumer. Here is a high-end brand in the auto market, and the footwear market is selling it with a completely different focus.

Imagine Jeep, the car company, selling its automobiles to the middle and upper-end markets, but the bags and strollers are selling in the lower-end market. Where is the logic in that? Doesn't that create a conflict in consumer perception? If I owned a Jeep, thinking it was a higher-end product, and I learned about or saw the extended products in discount stores, it would change my perception of the brand. Without communicating the essence of the brand across all divisions, you risk confusing your customers and possibly destroying the integrity of your brand, which you may have spent years developing and maintaining.

How are the consumers to know that these products are made by an offshoot of some other company? They are not going to know that, and that is why it is even more important to manage your brand well when licensing out your name. The consumer has no idea in most cases that a product is produced by some other company and that it is not associated directly with yours. More and more consumers are learning and believing that a product bearing one name is one brand and one company. Thus, what happens outside with your name is just as powerful as what happens inside your name.

Many of us in business tend to think others know what we know or, even worse, think that others will ask or learn what they need to know. The first thing you should do is stop, look around, and decide who and what you are. Decide how you are going to get where you want to be and find the best way to communicate that. Make sure that the people within and around your organization are aware of the roots of your business, what you do today, and what the plans are for tomorrow.

EXTERNAL EDUCATION

External education is critical. If you're a manufacturer or product manager, you must educate your distributors and retailers. If you're not educating the people who are interfacing with your customers and those who are interacting with the ultimate consumer of your product, you're putting yourself behind the eight ball. You cannot and should not rely on retailers to get the word out when it comes to communicating or educating the consumer about your message.

Retailers today are focused on driving consumers into their stores. They are spending the vast majority of their advertising dollars on promoting their stores, their store brands, and sales. More and more retailers rely on promotional pricing as the lead driving motivator for consumers, and the consumers love it. The consumers have done a great job of educating the retailers that they will buy the product when it is on sale, and so the retailer reacts and promotes quite frequently, partly by necessity to drive sales volume and partly in response to pressure from outside forces such as the financial community and the press to react in a similar fashion to the way others may be promoting. As goes one retailer, so go so many others. This is particularly evident at key selling periods such as the holiday season.

Look at what happens when one retailer breaks price and promotes. Others have to follow suit. The retail giant Wal-Mart went into holiday season 2004 trying to be less promotional. Wal-Mart reported sluggish sales for the month of November because it chose to be less promotional. Wal-Mart's competition responded by out-Wal-Marting Wal-Mart by offering lower prices on key categories and products. Consumers reacted very methodically and shopped for the items and categories they desired at the retailers that offered the best prices. Wal-Mart then adjusted its strategy and for the latter part of December went promotional by reducing its prices to compete. The result? Wal-Mart returned to a healthier sales number of 3 percent growth for the same stores for the month of December compared with the prior year, ending with 2 percent sales growth for the same stores for the holiday season of November and December. Thus, educating yourself and your company about the focus, the goal, and the heritage is critical. Operating in a vacuum as Wal-Mart did in holiday season 2004 is not the way to go. It is not about what you think alone; it is what the consumer thinks as well.

You must communicate the essence of your brand yourself. Relying on others to communicate the essence of your brand is risky business. Retailers are focused on driving traffic and promoting themselves, and so they concentrate on promoting their sales and house brands. Think about how much time, energy, and money is being spent promoting the brands that are store-centric. Target does a terrific job of marketing private brands directly to the consumer, including Isaac Mizrahi, Cherokee, and Mossimo, among others.

If you are not one of these national brands selling to Target, can you really rely on the store to market to the consumer? Can you rely on the sales associates to communicate the essence and value of your brands and products? Probably not. As we enter a more self-service-oriented retail environment, you must find a way to make your product speak for itself.

Helping your product speak for itself is all about packaging. It is important to find ways to do things that are sometimes as simple as writing the benefits of the product on the box or the hang tag. Imagine a pair of boots that have steel toes for safety but do not mention this feature. How is a consumer to know? But if you have a hang tag explaining the benefits of the steel toe and other features of the boot, that allows the product to speak for itself. A car dealer wouldn't think of just putting a car on the sales floor and locking it up without a salesperson to showcase the features, a beautiful brochure to display the options and colors, and even a test drive to feel it out. How can a consumer know what a product does unless it is stated explicitly?

So many times I see products, such as shoes that come in a box, that the consumer must touch at some point. What a great opportunity to communicate a message of some sort: benefits, the image of the brand, or something else. Don't let that space go to waste. How about a talking hang tag? Yes, a talking hang tag. That is a great way to communicate a message in a few words that can be as powerful as or more powerful than a sales associate in some stores selling a product. Imagine being able to place a hang tag the size of a business card on a product that voices its benefits with a recorded message. Wouldn't you pay a dollar more to get your message across in such a way?

The men's skin-care market is an excellent example of methods for educating consumers. The recent growth in the beauty business is being fueled by new fragrance launches and men's cosmetics and skin care. Yes, men's skin care. As Fig. 8-2 shows, men's skin care has grown to a $52 million business in the United States at retail, which is a 10 percent increase for 2003 and 8 percent over the last 12 months. Furthermore, 32 percent of men under 30 years of age state that they are unhappy with their complexion. One out of three already is telling the industry that he is looking for help.

FIGURE 8-2 Men's cosmetics, dollar sales in department stores in millions of dollars by year. Men's prestige cosmetics continue to grow, even though they are not new.

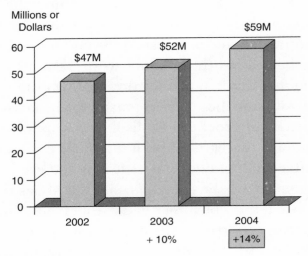

SOURCE: NPD Group.

What makes this work is that the men's skin-care industry, much the way the Dairy Association did, has recognized the need to educate consumers on the value of the products. Not every guy is willing to risk his macho aura and try on skin-care products, let alone be seen sitting on a stool in a department store getting a makeover.

How did the men's skin-care industry tackle this issue? It educated consumers on the benefits by getting men to read about and learn about the products through magazine and website articles and by running advertising in the appropriate places to make grooming and skin-care products within their comfort zone. To do this, businesses utilized the media, getting magazines to write articles about the benefits of skin care. They offered writers the ability to test the products, communicated the benefits of those products through in-store demonstrations, and made the most of word-of-mouth initiatives. Men shifted their social conversations from the traditional "did you see that game last night?" to include or even focus on what to wear to a client meeting, where to shop for the right clothes, and what products work for grooming. Men today constantly are trying to find out the appropriate style of attire for particular business and social events. Without an education effort that went directly to the consumer, this growth rate would have been nonexistent.

Educating your customer about what your product does should be one of the most important priorities both in product development and in marketing. Your message can get distorted the same way it gets distorted in the game of telephone, in which kids pass a message from person to person and by the time it goes through all the parties, it ends up flat-out wrong. Well, it's the same for your product. If you are going to rely on others to carry your product's message, something is going to get lost and little if any of your original message is going to get through.

ELEVATE

Consumers today are spending their discretionary dollars on items that will improve their quality of life. We discussed some of the reasons for this trend in Chapter 1. Whether it is with the purchase of a new flat-screen, high-definition television or that of a new kitchen with granite countertops and high-end appliances, consumers are looking to step up. Replacement is only one part of the equation, but in today's technologically aggressive and quickly changing world, obsolescence is quickly making upgrades more important.

Will the programs we watch be any better on a plasma set? With cable offering over 100 channels, will there be anything good to watch? Probably not, yet consumers are demonstrating that they are willing to pay big dollars in excess of $1,800 for a new plasma or LCD TV or $100 a month for cable. Sales of new enhanced televisions grew at a rate of nearly 100 percent in 2004, yielding $2 billion in sales of plasma and LCD televisions. Interestingly, sales of these television sets, particularly advanced ones, spike around Super Bowl time. Many consumers want to entertain family and friends with the "best set on the block" and elevate the experience of the event.

Another industry that clearly understands and demonstrates the importance of elevating the consumer and its product mix is the auto industry. Car companies have been trying to elevate product and in turn consumers for decades. In just the last two years, Cadillac has redefined what it is and refined who its customer is with the introduction of cars that are targeted to a younger, sportier, more performance-oriented and even status-seeking consumer. Think back to when Cadillac was the premium car on the road. You have to go back to the 1960s to see this, a time when those fins really meant something. Over the years, with the increase in imports and the shift toward European vehicles with the prestige and allure of luxury, Cadillac went down the path of steady market share declines, to the point where the cars were bought only by the "little old ladies from Pasadena" who "only drove to their place of worship once a week." As was discussed earlier, Cadillacs are being purchased by younger consumers for their gritty style, by status seekers for their urban ruggedness and luxury, and by the midsector market for their ability to elevate the driver with great enhancements and style all in one package.

Automakers are doing something that is very important. They are willing to take the brand and offer levels of product. Just a few years ago you couldn't get a luxury European car for under $45,000 in the United States. Today Mercedes, Land Rover, Jaguar, and BMW have sedans for less than $30,000, as do other manufacturers. Why? Dropping the price opens up an opportunity for the consumer to experience the brand. Some people argued that this was a terrible move by the European automakers, that they would be diluting the essence of their brands.

Critics felt that consumers who had spent $60,000 and up would be insulted seeing Mercedes cars on the road that cost under $30,000. But sales of the higher-priced vehicles have not diminished at all, and the market share of these brands has increased across a wider range of consumers. Young and less wealthy consumers aspiring to own a Mercedes, Land Rover, or Jaguar now can have that experience earlier in life and eventually trade up or elevate to a new experience, a new aspirational purchase, and become loyal consumers for a much longer period. Even if they never achieve the higher status of being able to afford the ultra-luxury sedans, they now have a piece of luxury right there in their hands.

Offer the consumers a path to elevate their lifestyle. Give them a reason to buy something that will make them feel good about their purchase and help them express their emotions in such a way that their hard-earned income allows them to move up and feel like they are getting somewhere.

Why do consumers trade up in housing? Why do they sell and move up? Just getting started on the housing merry-go-round is critical to becoming a part of this elevating consumer behavior. Many of us beg, borrow, and mortgage our lives up to our eyeballs just to get started with owning a home. The average American family is on the move within seven years. Sometimes it's because of job relocation, but more often it is done to elevate to a bigger or better home. Selling the family home can be due to something as simple as seeking to elevate one's living in a better school district or neighborhood.

How does your product help consumers elevate their everyday lives? You need to think about communicating to your consumers that your product will elevate them to a new plateau. What does your product offer them? Why should they purchase it? What will it do for them? How will it help them elevate in life? More important, why should they eventually replace it and get rid of what they already have? So much of what is bought today consists of replacements: trade-ups. In this case, elevating is the critical message. Why go from cable television to satellite? What will the benefits be? Financial, quality, product offering, and variety are all good points to highlight, and your message must contain some or all of these elements.

Whether you are selling skin-care products or automobiles, the ultimate question is, What is this going to do for the consumers? How are you communicating the message that you are helping them make more out of their lives, their purchases, and their status? Consumers demonstrate time and time again their desire to buy something that will change or enhance their lives, and you have to tap into that desire. Elevating them is an important part of that and a message too big to be ignored.

ELEVATE THROUGH THE COMMUNITY

The ability to elevate a brand through involvement in the community is a powerful way to convert consumers into the loyal ones we all seek in business and relationships. Look at what Wal-Mart has done to move beyond the negative publicity it gets. It does a lot in regard to community events and charities. Wal-Mart is viewed as the big bad giant, but it does a lot of goodwill work and even takes some old stores and converts them into community centers or donates the space to other needy causes when those stores move into bigger and more modern locations. And it advertises along these lines to counter the bad press.

Even if you aren't as big as Wal-Mart, and one would be hard-pressed to find many companies that are, you can utilize the idea of elevating your brand through the community. Sponsor events at schools or local playhouses. Help build skateboard parks or recreation centers. Bring your brand to the consumer to show that you care. Let consumers respond by endorsing your product by purchasing it on the basis of that relationship. You will be amazed at how powerful word of mouth is at the local level.

Timberland, for example, is in partnership with more than a dozen community organizations. In one case Timberland and Home Depot teamed up to build houses for the needy in local communities. Home Depot donates the building supplies, and Timberland supplies clothing for the volunteers. The power of this kind of activity is huge for brand recognition.

ENTERTAIN

Entertaining the consumer is the secret formula that seals the deal. We talked about entertainment brands and celebrity spokespersons earlier in the book and the value celebrities add to an offering in the mind of the consumer.

But let's not forget that you can use the actual shopping experience as well as a product's features as a vehicle for entertaining the customer.

ENTERTAINING THE CONSUMER IN THE FORM OF SHOPPING

When consumers set out to shop, they are making a commitment of their precious time. They are using their leisure time, and so they're making a conscious decision to go to the movies, spend time with friends, or go shopping. Whether they're shopping online or in stores, it is leisure time they are using for that experience, and so you must make it entertaining and fun for them. If consumers dread shopping, which many have learned to do, you need to find ways to make it fun again. Certainly the Internet has made it more convenient, but that taps into only a certain percentage of consumers. Although dollar sales remain relatively small on the Internet as a percentage of purchases for many industries, it has become a very powerful tool for shopping. Purchasing is one thing; shopping for information (education) and entertainment is another. Learn why consumers are using your website (you *do* have a website, don't you?) and make it more engaging for them.

People give considerable thought to making an actual purchase (although their impression of the product is formed almost instantaneously). With less time shopping and more diversified spending, it is critical that you engage the consumer by making shopping fun, easy, and informative, that is, entertaining. Advertising has tapped into this with humorous campaigns for decades, but the relationship with the product has gone beyond tickling the funny bone. Consumers expect the product to perform and to

keep their interest. It is no longer enough to offer a white mixer for the kitchen countertop. Consumers now look for the added functions of color and entertainment.

KitchenAid understands this and offers its heavy-duty mixer in a wide array of colors. Even for those who never intend to use the mixer, it makes a great statement and is entertaining to look at, like a piece of art on the countertop. LG, formerly Goldstar Electronics, understands the importance of entertainment and has introduced a refrigerator that has a built-in television in the door.

Entertaining consumers while they are shopping and purchasing extends to usage as well. Consumers are learning very rapidly that investing their discretionary spending across industries that entertain them makes those dollars spent last a long time. We are seeing a decrease in hobbies and an increase in collecting. Look at where the growth is coming from. Other than food, many industries are about collecting or entertaining. The iPod phenomenon, the continuation of consumers purchasing movies on DVDs, and the growth in personal and portable entertainment products are indications that entertainment is a valued element in purchase priorities today. When I asked 31,000 consumers to prioritize their spending interests—meaning, when it comes to spending your money, where do you rate the categories in order of priority?—it was no surprise that consumer electronics rose right to the top for men and was a close second for women, behind health and fitness (see Fig. 8-3).

Keep in mind that we are entering a world where the consumer is seeking entertainment both from the product and the experience. If your product makes that connection, you will be part of the future. If it does not, you will be working hard simply to survive.

FIGURE 8-3 Level of interest in spending by gender for various types of consumer goods. Figures shown indicate the percentage of male and female consumers who were either somewhat, very, or extremely interested in these categories, February–July 2004.

■ Males		
• Computers/Electronics	86%
• Health/Fitness	68%
• Car/Car Care	68%
• Home Furnishings	41%
• **Fashion**	**26%**
■ Females	
• Health/Fitness	75%
• **Computers/Electronics**	**71%**
• Home Furnishings	68%
• **Fashion**	**49%**
• Car/Car Care	48%

SOURCE: NPD Purchase Behavior Poll, involving 31,000 people.

EXPLORE

Consumer expectation studies can help you understand what the customer expects from the experience of using your brand, product, or service. For example, if someone orders something online or from a catalog or on the phone and that customer is informed that the item will ship the next day and he or she should expect to receive it within seven business days and then that item is at the door in three days, how do you think the customer is going to feel? If you establish a customer expectation with an acceptable standard and then exceed that expectation, you'll have happy customers who believe your brand or service has their best interests at heart. Learn what's expected by your customers and do whatever it takes to meet or exceed those expectations. You can't meet or exceed expectations if you don't know what they are.

I encourage all my clients to learn clearly and quickly what the expectations of a product or service are. You can accomplish this with something as simple as a follow-up survey that can be done by phone, in the mail, or online.

However, one of the best methods that I've mentioned throughout this book is the face-to-face interview. You should find unbiased consumers who would be potential consumers of your product. Introduce yourself and explain your mission. Have a set of questions that will help you learn from them what they would want from your product or service. You should ask what is important to them and thus how they would judge the product to be good, great, or not so good. Learning what they want, whether they were satisfied, and what they are looking for are all keys to connecting and successfully getting them as ambassadors for your product or service.

Just imagine a family that wants to hire a house painter. Do they expect the window trim to be painted along with the house? If they expect the trim to be painted and you don't know that, they will not be satisfied no matter how great a paint job you do. But if up front you knew the expectation was to get the trim painted, you would be able to deliver. Or you can hire a research firm to do this on a large or even a small scale. The trick is knowing what to ask, asking enough people, and staying consistent with your questions. Even the slightest difference can sway the results.

Let's go back to the person who ordered something from the catalog. Not only did the consumer get it sooner than

Learn what's expected by your customers and do whatever it takes to meet or exceed those expectations.

expected, let's say it came packaged in a way that also exceeded the customer's expectations. The product lived up to the hype in the copy and looked great. You can bet that consumer is going to be a mouthpiece for your brand or service, and as Mark Twain said, "I could live on one good compliment for a whole week." Well, brands can survive on something much like that. Word of mouth can make or break many companies. It is very easy to help influence the number of positive compliments for your brand, product, or service just by understanding the consumer's expectations. Learn them. Track them. And exceed them.

INNOVATION IS AN IMPORTANT PART OF EXPLORING

"New and improved" is a concept that's been around for a long time, but that doesn't mean it is not still powerful. Let's look at the men's pants business. Why would a guy need another pair of khakis? Well, according to consumers, the number one reason men buy a new pair of pants is to replace a pair that has worn out. The second most important reason: They don't fit anymore. The third reason is that they have an important meeting or event and need something to wear that is appropriate or acceptable. What does this all mean? It means that men by nature are going to buy a new pair of pants only when they have to.

Let's look at the life of a pair of khakis. The khakis are bought to wear to work. This works out for about a year provided that they don't get ripped or stained. They go from "wear to work" to the "weekend paint the house" role. When the pants went into the weekend stage, a replacement pair had to be purchased. So goes the average male apparel purchase cycle. Is that going to help pants manufacturers and retailers grow their business? No. Enter the importance of exploring ways to find other reasons for consumers to have to build their pants wardrobe. Give them a reason to buy a new pair of pants while the ones they have are still good enough. Enter wrinkle-free. Ah-hah! All of a sudden, both the male and the female in the household get a glimpse of this new innovation, and it stimulates their curiosity and they choose to learn more about this wrinkle-free product. Wow! Or maybe the stain-resistant feature captured his attention. No more stains means longer wear life, and hey, while we're here, why not pick up that tie you need?

Getting consumers to explore an innovative product can indeed raise sales for your brand and service. Consumers are willing to explore to find new and innovative products, as should you. Newness can fuel growth: Don't downplay the importance of this in motivating the consumer and driving the consumer toward your brand.

EXPLORE WAYS TO LET THE CONSUMER ENDORSE YOUR BRAND

A great example of the importance of exploring is provided by the success of a relatively small athletic footwear brand. The footwear company Merrell was able to score higher than the leading brand in brand relevance for all of its women's casual footwear. Women rated Merrell the number one brand that understands their lifestyle. Merrell did it by exploring new ways to communicate that message to its customers, utilizing its website to go beyond its core message and talk about lifestyle subjects. The company utilized hang tags and packaging in a more effective way and utilized word-of-mouth marketing better than almost anyone in the industry. Women found this shoe to be incredibly comfortable and practical and, above all, something that made their lives better. The shoe seemed to connect with them as no other shoe brand has. Women are very vocal about the love they have for this brand. They tell almost everyone they know and love to tell the story of the little footwear brand they feel they discovered.

Be bold when creating ways to communicate your brand message: product giveaways, products embossed with the brand names, hang tags. The list goes on.

What this is all about is letting the consumer endorse your brand. Word-of-mouth marketing is a very powerful tool. When you can get each of your consumers to shout your praises, you can bet you will reach the ears and minds of at least 10 new people through each of those consumers. Don't be shy about finding new and innovative ways to communicate your message. Begin doing this with each new season of planning or start today by exploring ways to get the word out about what your brand is and how it can connect with your ultimate consumer. Some ways to do this are as simple as providing additional information on the packaging or on hang tags. A fun way to explore how to become a more relevant brand is to offer a small gift with each purchase. The cosmetics industry has been doing this for years, and it works. It gives consumers greater value and introduces them to your new and innovative products.

Another effective way to get consumers to carry the torch for your brand is to provide them with products that carry the brand. A varsity backpack, the inexpensive kind that uses string for the straps and is flat and square, is a great example. Imagine if a footwear company wrapped its shoes in the box in these backpacks. The consumers would feel good about getting an extra item, and if they liked the product or, even better, loved it, they would be proud to carry that bag. Something as simple as a key chain or a hang tag bearing the brand or logo is an easy way to accomplish this. This is not a new concept by any means, but it may be new for you and your brand.

In the earlier days at my marketing company we developed all kinds of loyalty and reward programs to encourage more purchases and product endorsements by the ultimate consumer, including currencies for brands that consumers could collect to get great deals and reduced prices on products that matched their lifestyles beyond the core product. I called them brand extensions. We offered "Beam Bucks" to Jim Beam Bourbon consumers so that they could collect currency from events, magazines, and catalogs; included with the product; and even in stores, all with the intent to get consumers to try Jim Beam products beyond the main product, bourbon. Imagine a consumer feeling the desire to be loyal to the brand and getting rewarded for it. Now add the fact that you can get an additional product that fits in with your lifestyle and you have an even more loyal consumer who is willing to wear your product with pride. This is like a walking billboard for your brand. It doesn't get much better than this.

EVALUATE

The E links become a locked chain only if you evaluate your progress. The Five E's of marketing all come together when you Evaluate the performance. By taking the time to assess the progress of the other four E's—Educate, Elevate, Entertain, and Explore—you will be able to secure the chain. Take the time to make sure that all the links are solid. The chain is only as strong as its weakest link, as the saying goes. Although each link is not equally important, each is an integral part of the equation. Don't eliminate one link, but it is possible to minimize its importance as it relates to your business. Some programs may need to phase in the links one at a time, but it is critical to measure each link and determine if the marketing program is working effectively or is in need of modifications.

Many companies either wait too long to make shifts in marketing programs or don't give the programs enough time to materialize. I recall watching one company that was so quick to judge a marketing program that it never stopped to realize that the consumers didn't even receive their marketing pieces. They weren't willing to wait the amount of time needed for the consumers to catch up to the campaign. When I asked them if the consumers had received any of the pieces, they were shocked to learn that they hadn't. They never stopped to put a calendar of events together and were focused only on the budget calendar to make the decision.

This happens more often then you would think. Decisions are made on the basis of budgets, understandably, but during the evaluation stage it is critical to ensure that all the components are being viewed in the process. Don't pull the plug on a program that hasn't had time to affect the product or brand. It takes time for word of mouth to get around and even more time for the demand for the product to be timely for the second wave of communication to consumers. Although the first wave may have gotten the prod-

> Be patient: Don't cancel programs that haven't had time to affect the brand or product.

uct, the second wave needs time to absorb it, find the need, and create the demand. Be patient, be creative, be connected, and most of all be calculated.

EVALUATE THE PRODUCT FOR THE PRODUCT'S SAKE AS WELL

Hanes is a great example of a company that figured out how to evaluate its product. A division of Sara Lee Apparel, Hanes is now selling to a wide variety of retailers. The average men's underwear consumer doesn't really know the difference between the Hanes brands that are sold in department stores and mass merchants. But the need for a difference is there, as the price of the product is significant.

Hanes determined that it needed to create three tiers of product. One is Hanes Ultimates, a premium line that sells to higher-end stores and offers a finer grade of fabric and quality. This is a product that is limited to distribution mainly through the better stores such as department stores and the manufacturer's own website. It is a product that offers product differentiation, which is key to the department store channel. The company then added to the mix the Hanes Classics collection for the midtier stores. This is a product that you can find on the Sara Lee website, in the factory outlet stores, and at chain store retailers. For the mass merchant retailers, there is the Hanes brand. It offers them the opportunity to put price ahead of quality but not sacrifice the quality and integrity of the brand.

NOT ALL BRANDS CAN ROLL OUT 13 DIFFERENT SUBBRANDS

You should evaluate whether you want to roll out your products and services to a wider range of consumers and, while you are doing so, if the brand should remain constant. It's important to determine whether the brand can carry a subbrand that will separate it enough from the core brand without sacrificing the integrity.

Evaluate carefully as you examine the possibility of rolling out a product to a wider range of retailers or consumers. Not all brands can manage the process of creating 13 subbrands, as Ralph Lauren has done. Each Ralph Lauren brand has a clear purpose internally, but to the consumer there appears to be some dilution. How different is the Lauren brand from the Polo brand? How different is the Polo Jeans brand from the parent brand? It's not always clear to the consumer. Although the design team clearly knows and the brand managers most likely do, the line is blurred in the eyes of the consumer. With the brand power it has, the Lauren name in almost any form takes on a point of value. The true loyalist has Purple or Black label Ralph Lauren to choose, whereas the Ralph Lauren aspirational consumer can always choose from among Polo, Lauren, Polo Jeans, and Polo Sport. For the lower-end designer wannabe, they have Chaps by Ralph Lauren to get a taste of the upper-class brand family.

COMBINING ALL THE E'S

Apple Computers used all Five E's to make its iPod a total success. Apple educated consumers on the value of personal music. This was not new, but the MP3 format surely was. If the iPod had been viewed as just another Walkman or CD player, it never would have had the impact it did. Thus, educating the consumer and marketplace was step 1. Elevating consumers to take the plunge was step 2: getting them comfortable with the idea that this was a new and improved method of listening to and managing music. Tapping into the entertainment link was easy, as music is certainly a direct connection. For the exploration link, consider the speed at which they introduced new product, exploring ways to make the product more fun and relevant, and the way Apple has stayed ahead of the competition with the Mini models, a greater memory capacity, and Windows compatibility. They even explored ways to deliver the music to the consumer and started the iTunes Music Store, a website where consumers can purchase music to download to their iPods. And the iTunes Music Store offers a host of benefits and lifestyle features, from information to products. They offer fashion accessories and replacement parts, some from Apple and some from other brands jumping on the iPod wave.

When it came time to evaluate the product, Apple did. Early iPods had frustrated consumers because the battery life was too short. After an hour the unit would need to be recharged, and that did not make it travel-friendly and truly portable in the consumer's eyes. Lesson learned: They fixed the problem for the second-generation version. Apple evaluated how its iPod was being received, listened to complaints, and acted on them. The expectations of the consumers were different from those of the product makers, leading to some disappointment. Thus, even with the success of the product, the evaluation process initially fell short, Apple adjusted quickly with needed fixes and went on to have one of the greatest success stories in history.

Take the time to create your own chain of links for the Five E's of marketing and don't forget to evaluate along the way and lock in the success you need to propel your brand to the next level. This is an excellent way to communicate the path for the company and get your team headed in a direction that will connect with the consumer. After you do this, start all over again and update the links accordingly. But don't be premature in making adjustments. Let them play out and take their course and then evaluate them again, and you will see results.

9

MARKETING STRATEGIES OF THE FUTURE

WHAT IF I TOLD YOU that the way the majority of us visit the doctor is about to change or that those long lines at the airport are a thing of the past? Would you believe me? With a product that imitates the EZ Pass, you'll never be in waiting line Hell, either in the doctor's office or when waiting to board your flight. Professionals are testing an array of futuristic products and services in an effort to identify and shape emerging consumer trends. It is up to you to determine how to implement these trends and to recognize how to turn your business into a marketing machine. The Five E's will help you assess how current trends will evolve, create a vision for the future, and provide a strategy to go with it.

Less Is More...Doctor Doctor...Are you aware that there are an estimated 850,000 doctors in the United

States? Now, divide the population of the United States by the number of doctors and you end up with an average of 3,200 patients per doctor. Wow, that is a lot of patients in a year, isn't it? Think of the last visit you made to the doctor and recognize the amount of time you had to wait or even just get an appointment. On average the waiting time to see a doctor is close to an hour. Okay, so what is new about this? Nothing yet. But some doctor's offices are using a new system called MD VIP—where an elite core of doctors maintains an elite group of patients. Each doctor takes on only 300 patients, not 3,000. This allows each doctor to spend a half hour per visit on average and to give the patients more quality care, less of a factory assembly line process as sometimes occurs today. The patient has the doctor's cell phone number, there is no waiting and in fact no need to make an appointment. With only 300 patients that would average out to one patient a day in a year. They offer CDs with the history of the patient. They spend time to offer consultations and to network with other doctors to offer similar special care. This is the way of the future for many doctors who are frustrated with the level of care and the loss of personalization in medicine today. Doctors group together to share offices and staff, making the process more pleasurable, and in the process offer better and more personal care. Could you imagine, if you get a sore throat or rub up against some poison ivy, you'll no longer need to wait over a week to see your doctor just to get a culture taken to learn if it is strep throat, or some lotion to spread on that terrible itch that is driving you right out of your own skin?

What is in it for the doctors? Well, the doctors see 300 patients on a need-to basis, with each patient paying an annual fee of $1,500 per year. As a result, the doctors make the same money as before but have a much more meaningful relationship with their clients. This is clearly a win-win situation. Patients are happier and better cared for, and the doctors state they are more attentive to the patients' needs, live a better life, and are even more connected with their patients. What a great solution, happier and healthier people in the health care system. Not to mention those staffers in the doctors' offices. Maybe now they won't be so grumpy and overtaxed with paperwork and red tape. Not that the red tape will go away so quickly, but it will be a lot more manageable with a fixed number of patients. This is a great lesson in the benefits of simplifying or making less more.

WHATEVER HAPPENED TO FOCUSING ON TECHNOLOGY?

Take a look at where we are today when it comes to advertising for personal computers. In technology and computer sales, all the computer companies once focused on speed, ease of use, and convenience, but now the emphasis has shifted to price. It seems that speed is taken for granted, the processor on board is good enough, and the features in the computer are more about what it can do rather than how well. Consumers are either in the upgrade mode or the real late-bloomer mode when it comes to purchasing a computer (see Fig. 9-1). The other way to look at computer purchasers today is the first-time owner, not necessarily user, such as a student. These lend themselves to being users, but users on a budget. So the industry has taken the lead with consumers looking to purchase a second computer or for those that have hesitated for a long

FIGURE 9-1 Consumer category demographics: total PCs purchased for 12-month period ending May 2005.[*†]

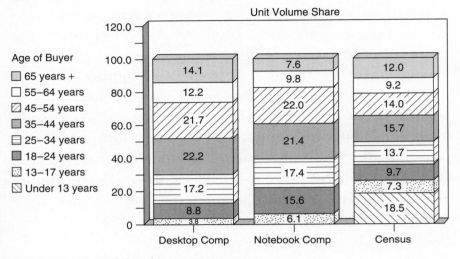

* Consumer panel data begins May 2001.
[†] Reported volumes represent purchased categories only.
SOURCE: NPD Group.

time and are now willing to step up and buy one because the price has become more affordable to their budget. We are seeing the average age of users and purchasers shifting slightly, and that in turn is creating the need to market differently with different features and pricing structures to lure consumers in.

PRICE, PRICE, PRICE

Have you ever stopped to think about how you will compete in the price wars that seem to exist in every product and service market today?

One glance at a newspaper or at a few commercials on television and you will be barraged with ads featuring how to save more than ever before. Just take one look at the cable vs. satellite television wars. Each is on the air and in the papers sporting its deal of the day. They use price and packaging as a tool to get your attention, and each promises the best value and the best viewing possible. Some even bundle services together offering incentive pricing if you sign up for all three. Cablevision in the Northeast is offering digital cable television, telephone service, including long distance along with high-speed internet access, all for the low price of $29.99 each if you purchase all three. Satellite TV is offering a different package claiming greatest value with lower prices and more channels. You can't pick up a newspaper or watch television and not see these ads barraging you with attempts to lure you to switch over and by using price as the lure. Some even go so far as to blatantly ask if you are tired of high cable bills.

How about the phone companies filling the airwaves, direct-mail campaigns, and newspapers with ads offering better value through long distance calling packages. Some companies bundle them into packages providing both local and long distance calling. Just think of how many times you have seen James Earl Jones stepping into your living room talking about phone plans for Verizon, but what is he really offering? Such offers are becoming just noise to the average consumer. Sometimes the message may be different, but the dynamics of the offer aren't that different, and consumers tune them out as if they have heard such offers over and over again. It might very well be the perfect plan for the viewer or reader, but because they have seen the face and brand before, they half listen.

Now look at the phone companies for cellular service. Wow, talk about price offerings and constant commercials, these companies are sure to be something you get to see and hear about several times a day. Have any of these ad executives stopped to think about how difficult it is for a consumer to weed through all the offerings? Walkie Talkie phones, picture phones, free phones, rollover minutes, unlimited calling between 7 p.m. and 7 a.m., and even waiting for no long distance charges after 8 p.m.— all are touch points, but when a consumer sees them all, over and over again, it becomes overwhelming. Maybe one point will get through, but then it is over. That issue was the deciding factor, but to keep competing based on price is not the only answer. That is why you see so many phone companies using celebrities to send the message; it allows them to establish an identity. Here is a pop quiz. Are you ready? What cellular phone company uses Catherine Zeta Jones as their spokesperson? And what is it that she is selling in their ads? While you may get the name of the company right, T-Mobile, the odds are overwhelming you have no idea what offer she is pitching. It takes a lot of patience to weed through all the offerings and select a plan, not to mention picking the right cellular phone carrier for you. Most people just settle on the phone they like or the company that delivers the best service in their area.

My favorite current trend to cite as a method of marketing for the future these days is the auto industry—talk about Price, Price, Price. Take a look at where we are today with the auto industry. You have GM trying to sell more cars in June as their inventory is backing up. They offer the first-time-ever Employee Discount Prices for Everyone campaign. They do a great job of mixing in the price offering with displaying the pride they have with their employees stating they work in the number one, two, and three factories in the GM stable. The idea here is to make it look like this discount they are about to tell you about is a good thing, not merely a surplus inventory sale. The commercial goes on to say "Each and every person today can buy a GM car today at the employee discount price." They make it sound as if it is because we the average consumer did something so great to make GM the biggest car company in the United States that they are offering us this great deal. Well, I guess you could say that is true. We buy the cars, and that in some way makes them the biggest car company in the United States. But is that really the reason we deserve a discount?

GM does very well with this campaign. In fact, they get a 50 percent bump in June sales. They decide to extend the offer into July to expire on August 1. Now what happens? Chrysler and Ford offer up their employee discount programs to offset the drop they have and to combat the offering GM made. Chrysler goes so far as to bring back its legendary former Chairman and CEO Lee Ioacocca regarded as the force behind Chrysler's success a decade earlier. This was not without controversy by the way, as Ioacocca left Chrysler on some shaky terms by endorsing the group that was attempting a takeover bid. So instead of focusing on the products as they usually do, the focus shifts to price. The consumer now has the choice of almost any American-made car at the so-called Employee Discount price. How is this different from when we saw 0% financing only just a few years earlier? Not much, in that price is the real underlying message here. Just the packaging is being changed. It all comes down to Price, Price, Price.

LET'S TAKE A WALK...

Take a walk down the beverage aisle in a grocery store and
what do you see? Salespeople see an ocean of soft drinks
that are lined up like soldiers ready to refresh. The consumer sees something a bit different than that. Sure, there
are those that are brand loyal to their favorite cola or non-
cola. But the interesting thing about cola and some other
flavors are that they are price driven not brand driven. One
of the biggest determinations of which 2-liter bottle a consumer will purchase is which one is offered that week at 99
cents. And the price discounts are coordinated so sales by
brand don't compete with one another. Rarely do you see
both Coke and Pepsi offered at the 99 cent price in the
same week. They are used in circulars to lure consumers
in. Like a magnet, when the consumer sees the 2-liter sale
price they grab that bottle with the 99 cent sticker or shelf
talker, the extra tag hanging off the shelf promoting the
price or special of the day. So the next time you enter a grocery store, take a moment to look at the beverage aisle and
learn how important price really is. These soft drink companies wouldn't be giving away the margin if the pricing
game wasn't really important and effective. Would you
switch your brand of cola? Maybe not, but when it comes
time to managing the household budget, almost any cola
will do, especially when it comes at less than half the price.

SPEAKING ABOUT 99 CENTS...

Even the popular 99-cent meals are starting to fade since
the fast-food chains got into the price wars game. The
value meals or 99-cent menus began popping up every-

where. Wendy's, McDonald's, Burger King, and others are utilizing the 99-cent meal to talk about value and price. Taco Bell has joined in, along with Kentucky Fried Chicken, all in response to each other's attempt to offer value. Fill up for less than 99 cents boasts Taco Bell. Get real chicken for only 99 cents at Kentucky Fried Chicken. Each uses its own way to convey the message, but the message is the same: 99 cents will get you something to eat. These 99-cent meals are moving over, making way for the new, oversized food items like Hardees Monster Thickburger, for example, because price price price is becoming just noise. What happened to the campaign about healthier choices? What happened to the campaign about doing good things for the community? Many have been sidelined or scaled back.

How to retain customers sometimes is just as important, if not more important, than getting new ones. And if consumers are willing to switch due to price, the soft drink market, the fast-food industry, the cell phone industry, the automotive industry, and certainly the enhanced television industry, all show signs of vulnerability to brand loyalty and a quest for value by the consumer. Whether it is demonstrated with the success of a retailer like Target offering fun fashion at great prices, or a specialty retailer like American Eagle offering better value and still cool imagery for the teen, the consumer has learned that price is a way to select. And when the price is addressed head on by the brands and in marketing—they react. GM had to continue the Employee Discount Program, and it was so successful that Chrysler and Ford both had to respond, for more reasons than just short-term sales drops. They had to respond to retain those loyal customers that were due for a new car and try to keep them from even considering about shifting brands. The lesson here is not only to grow the brands through pricing but to retain your customer base. We live in a world today where price can no longer be ignored in the vast majority of products sold. And when your messaging is not about price, you need to be very clear as to why your product is needed, or is better than the competition. No longer should you take for granted that you have the best; someone, somewhere is nipping at your heels, waiting to capitalize on your success and deliver a similar product for less money. Now either go out and compete for price or sell the message that yours is better and why. Make sure you convey why your product or service is needed and what the benefits are.

CONNECTION MARKETING

Take notice of a great ad campaign being introduced by Dove. They call it "Real Beauty." They are using "real people," not models, to convey that beauty is more than skin deep. They have searched the country to find over 30 women that are being featured in their ads and on their website to show how their products address cosmetic and personal care issues important to women. They are testimonials about how the new line of new Dove products has transitioned their skincare, hair care, facial and body needs. They are doing this by picturing these women in nothing more than their undergarments. Yes, real women, not models, featured in ads wearing nothing more than a white bra and panty telling their story of what product they used by Dove and what it did for them—smiling for the entire world to see and baring it all, well practically all.

The power of this message is so strong that it has created quite the buzz in the media (an added bonus when it comes to getting consumers to recognize the advertising program).

But even without the media coverage, these ads stand out. Imagine walking in a mall, and seeing a life-size photograph of a woman in her bra and panty who is not stick thin, in fact not thin at all. You take notice for whatever reason and you see her personality come right through with a shy smile and story to tell. You take notice. If she can bare almost all and want to tell you about what this product did for her, you are willing to listen—and it is working. Dove is known primarily for its soap or, as they now say, cleansing cream.

Dove has found a new way to tap into the minds and hearts of consumers. By introducing an array of beauty products that are at more affordable prices and by addressing a wide variety of beauty needs for women, Dove has connected big time. What was perceived as products only available to those consumers that can afford to shop at department stores or specialty stores for these enhanced beauty and personal care products, Dove has addressed the same needs for the average gal at more affordable prices. People are relating to the women in these ads. From the ones with gray hair or wrinkles, or freckles, or even those who are slightly overweight, these women are real; and they are touching the hearts of women consumers.

"Finally a product campaign that I can relate to," is what I hear over and over again when I interview consumers and ask about the ads. Many consumers tell me that they don't like the in-store product demonstrations as a sales approach. They cite things such as pressure to buy products that either don't do enough for the price or don't work for them. Some even admit to buying things they really didn't want but felt "guilty" not buying after they had spent time with a cosmetologist in the store. Whatever the reason, this campaign has caught the attention and has connected with women in a way few campaigns have ever done. This is a program that will be looked at by not only the competition, but other industries as well. Look for more of these real campaigns to emerge in the future, it's not so much about image, it's about what real people, real products, and real prices can communicate.

Now, add in the potential of word of mouth and you have an even more powerful message. The Dove real beauty campaign strikes the chord that offers consumers the ability and desire to share their story. The power of word of mouth with products and services is one of the most important influences on consumers. This campaign provides not only the fodder for the consumer, but the desire to share it as well. Not only did Dove offer a great ad campaign, they extended the connection with offerings for consumers to connect with the products and issues on their website. Product knowledge, information, real stories, real people, and a place to chat about it, offers an even more rewarding experience and educational home for women trying to look and feel better. The website offers detailed information about what are the right products for your particular need. For instance, for oily hair, click on hair; choose your specific concerns and issues, and learn what to do and what the right range of products are for you. Whether it is your skin, your hair, or your face, Real Beauty has something to share with you. Each concern has a designated icon to click on, along with other icons encouraging consumers to share their thoughts and questions in the website's "we're listening" section.

REMEMBER WHEN THE PRIZE WAS BIGGER THAN THE SNACK?

Cracker Jacks made quite a mark for themselves by selling "popcorn, peanuts and prize, that's what you get in cracker jacks." I recall, just like every other kid opening the package from the bottom to get to the prize first, finding that the prizes got cheaper and cheaper. Gone were the decoder rings and compasses, and today the prize is a flip book or temporary tattoo. Yet that same excitement is not lost.

I'm finding that stores are experimenting with adding the prize back into the equation again. Look at the success of the Happy Meal at McDonald's and the toy program at Burger King. Some kids are more interested in going to get the toy than the meal itself. Clever, hah? Well, move over McDonald's, as one leading specialty apparel retailer is utilizing a play right out of the same book. How many kids will go shopping for a new swim suit and say when they see one, they must have it? Not many. But add a toy on it like a diver's watch that tells you how deep you are in the pool, from 2 to 10 feet. Or how about a treasure chest wallet that is nothing more than a plastic container to hold not much more than a few dollar bills or a tiny seashell. Attach these or other items on swimsuits or other apparel items and watch the item go from "its okay," to "I have to have that Mom." While this is not a new concept, remember laundry detergent that would offer a plate in the box, gas stations that would offer a drinking glass with the local football team with any fill up of 8 dollars or more, yes, 8 dollars. How about the cereal business that had kids reaching inside the box of cereal all the way up to their elbows just trying to find the prize inside, do you remember that? Well, even if you don't, you will become familiar with a lot of these gift-with-purchase opportunities popping up in lots

of new and not-so-new places. The thrill of the hunt, the
Wonka Bar golden ticket will return. And now we even have
Wonka brand candy on the shelves in stores everywhere.
Talk about having marketing being driven by entertainment, isn't it ironic how Wonka Bars are now in stores just
in time to coincide with the recent release of the adaptation of *Charlie and the Chocolate Factory*.

Hidden treasures are popping up in more and more
places. And it is not just the warehouse clubs that are taking advantage of adventure shopping. Another brand that
got this concept is Buster Brown; selling kids shoes with
super bounce balls included in the shoe box as an added
attraction and lure for kids. The child might not even like
the shoes, but they want the super bounce ball and are
willing to accept Mom's purchase of the style. Sometimes,
what was old is new again.

TIME TO THINK

Direct TV is offering the ability to not only get more digital channels, but they are also asking you to "ReThink TV."
They are offering free installation, free DVD player/
recorders featuring the TIVO technology and featuring a
new program they call Move Connection. Move Connection allows those that have Direct TV to be able to get free
installation if they move to a new location. What Direct
TV is telling consumers is that it is not the same anymore.
It is time to move up and aspire to have a more enhanced
television experience—and with the hassles taken out.
Direct TV is trying to utilize some of the 5 E's such as *elevate*, by offering the consumer enhanced products and
better television experiences. Direct TV is exploring ways
to keep customers by offering the Move Connection to

retain those that already have a dish and are getting ready to move to a new home. Direct TV is attempting to play the entertainment card by displaying the fact that they offer 300 channels compared to less from cable.

Another great example is seen in the insurance business. Look at what Geico offers: 15 minutes will save you 15% on your car insurance. Now look at how Progressive Insurance combats that. Progressive makes the *experience* that much better, choosing not to compete on price, but by educating the consumer on why service and knowledge is better and more important. They talk about how they will come to you, even arrive at the scene of the accident to support your needs. They talk about beginning your claims within 24 hours. Where Geico wants you to remember them with their Gecko lizard and appeal to your quest for value and savings by pounding away at creating happiness with fun commercials on how a congressional member at a hearing was excited when he saved a bunch on his car insurance. Geico has chosen to play the value card and the entertainment card. While others have chosen to ramp up their offerings and service to make the experience that much more pleasurable, this trend of fighting back in a nondirect way is the way we will see many brands and services begin to appeal to consumers that are displaying a desire for better than average and certainly better than cheap.

MORE AND MORE STORES SEEK OUTSIDE BRANDS TO ELEVATE PRODUCT OFFERINGS

Don't be surprised when you walk into some of your favorite retailers and discover they are selling more brands. Private Branded retailers that make their own products and use their store names will soon be reaching out toward other well-known brands to enhance their product assortments. So you will find that stores like Lane Bryant, known for their own brand of plus size women's clothing will be offering national brands like Seven Jeans and Danskin Activewear. No longer will it be only Lane Bryant product. Even the big status brand for teens, Abercrombie & Fitch, has plans to toy with this multiple-brand strategy.

Take a look at the food industry and how the store front has changed to multibrand platforms. That is a fancy way of saying you can now go to a Dunkin' Donuts and find many that have a Baskin Robbins Ice Cream shop in the same location. More and more cobranding will pop up as brands and retailers learn how to create synergy with brands to afford them to coexist and take advantage of the economies of scale for costs.

The other big trend to watch out for is the likelihood that brands will be inventing subbrands to market more exclusive offerings to retailers to separate them from competing retailers. So don't be surprised if you see more of the concepts like Chaps by Ralph Lauren available at Kohl's, while the Ralph Lauren brand will be offered at your local department store. This brand separation allows the retailers to distinguish their personality through branding and minimize the need to promote to stay competitive on the same brands.

WHAT WOULD YOU PAY FOR A PAIR OF 0.3-CARAT DIAMOND EARRINGS?

In a study done by another research firm, it was demonstrated that when a consumer is given the ability to offer up a price based on the following description, they came up with an average reply. Here is the description and the reply.

> How much would you pay for a pair of good quality, 0.3-carat diamond earring studs?

The answer was $521.00.

Now put a brand name to it and ask the same question with the brand name in the question.

> How much would you pay for a pair of good quality, 0.3-carat diamond earrings studs from Tiffany?

The answer was $831.00.

Now ask the same question with a different level of retail branding and see the power of branding.

> How much would you pay for a pair of good quality, 0.3-carat diamond earring studs from Wal-Mart?

The answer was $97.00.

If that doesn't exemplify the power of branding to you, read it again. Watch as we enter into a stage in consumer behavior that will be willing to pay more for brands that have prestige and aspiration associated with them. The luxury market will get more luxurious and the lower end of the market will get more luxurious but at amazingly different prices. The middle level brands and retailers will find ways to also market upward and downward, dividing their own brand(s) to seek the upper end of their market or the lower end.

Take one look at what Adidas did by offering a pair of running shoes for $250. Yes, $250 for a pair of running shoes. Sure these shoes help you run faster and jump higher and even adjust to the terrain via a computer chip under the sole by making the heel more firm or softer.

While this technology is not for everyone, the ultimate goal is the power that the brand receives by being the leader in technology in their market. Even if Adidas doesn't sell a single pair of these Adidas 1, as they are called, they are still ahead of the game with helping to transform or elevate their brand into the technologically advanced products offered by the likes of the behemoth Nike. So with all the Soul searching done at Adidas to compete with Nike, they have utilized exploring, elevating and educating in enhancing their brand perception. And not to stop there, they are continuing to introduce new and innovative products with their A3 line of air-cushioned system shoes. Talk about trying to be a step ahead, look at the energy they put forth in developing new products through technology even in running shoes.

Another important trend emerging is the growth in, what I call, "emerging channels." These are stores and even brands that are on the rise but not traditional ones. In apparel, look at the growth of stores and the Internet as places consumers are feeling more and more confident in shopping and purchasing from. Here is one statistic that might surprise you. Did you know that 55 percent of consumers have shopped in a dollar store in the past 12 months while comparing that to 38 percent of consumers that have shopped at moderate department stores. Yes, you read that right, there are substantially more consumers that have purchased from dollar stores than have purchased from moderate department stores. And the number just keeps on growing. (See Fig. 9-2.) Income levels would make a difference here, but not to the extent you would think. Upper-income shoppers are the fastest-growing segment to shop in value and treasure hunt stores like warehouse clubs and dollar stores. So even the upper-income households are out seeking value and in places traditionally never set foot in earlier. Watch as other emerging channels in categories make their mark in selling new categories. Home improvement centers have been expanding product offerings over the years and soon at a Home Depot or Lowe's near you there will likely be apparel and even footwear. Home Depot will be testing convenience stores in their parking lots to capitalize on the traffic and one-stop shopping experience for their consumers. How can you evolve your brand to make it easier for your consumer but not sacrifice all that you stand for? Look inside and outside your four walls for growth. Maybe you too have a convenience store in your future. Or maybe you too can find a way to sell a smaller version of your product to appeal to the dollar stores. By the way, not all dollar stores sell things for only a dollar. Visit one sometime and you may be quite surprised.

DEAR OL' MOM...

And yet one other trend that takes us back in time is marketing to Moms. Yes, Moms. Watch as brands and stores begin to try to talk to Moms again—Moms that work and don't work. Stores are beginning to realize they abandoned them and need to get them back. Moms are viewed as the hub of the household and in many cases the key purchase decision maker for many categories of business. So don't be surprised by all the focus in marketing in trying to get back the Mom and not just the young ones either. Motherhood is cool. Moms are not like they used to be and, with that, make for great marketing tools in today's world. These

FIGURE 9-2 Outlets shopped for any items in the past 12 months.

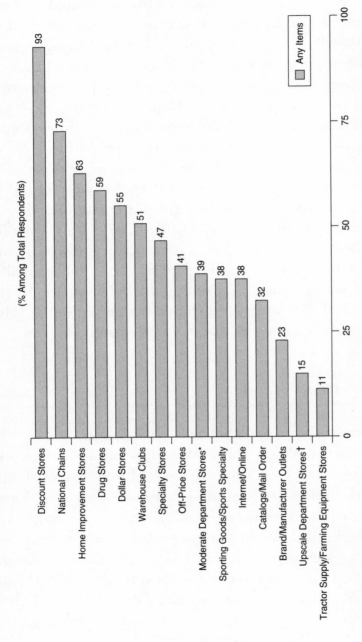

(% Among Total Respondents)

Discount Stores — 93
National Chains — 73
Home Improvement Stores — 63
Drug Stores — 59
Dollar Stores — 55
Warehouse Clubs — 51
Specialty Stores — 47
Off-Price Stores — 41
Moderate Department Stores* — 39
Sporting Goods/Sports Specialty — 38
Internet/Online — 38
Catalogs/Mail Order — 32
Brand/Manufacturer Outlets — 23
Upscale Department Stores† — 15
Tractor Supply/Farming Equipment Stores — 11

☐ Any Items

* Moderate Department Stores category is defined as Macy's, Rich's, Goody's, Bon Marche, Dillard, Belk, Filene's, etc.
† Upscale Department Stores category is defined as Nordstroms, Neiman Marcus, Saks, Bergdorf Goodman, Bloomingdale's, etc.
SOURCE: NPD Group.

are not Leave it to Beaver Moms, June, or even Murphy Brown type Moms. These are Miranda, Sex in the City Moms who will be shaping brands targeting women.

The future of tomorrow is being tested today. Keep your eyes open to elevate and explore your brand's potential. Look outside your own domain and evaluate the potential for these techniques. Educate, Explore and Expand.

10

AN ACTION PLAN FOR FULFILLING CUSTOMER ASPIRATIONS

I HOPE I HAVE DELIVERED on the promises made in this book's introduction. As you read this last chapter, you should have a good understanding of the latest trends in consumer behavior and the dynamics that are changing our industry as well as a system for fulfilling and even exceeding your customers' *aspirations*. In my view, the most important developments for brand managers and businesses in general are the focus on lifestyle as opposed to age and the notion of customer aspirations rather than expectations. These developments present great opportunities for shaping your brand, business, and product line but are also difficult concepts to wrap strategies and marketing tactics around.

As you craft your brand message, use the Five E's to help you meet the challenges of a changing marketplace brought on by the thinning middle, shifts in how value is defined, and the Sea of Sameness. Tap into the things that inspire and motivate your customers even if they don't have a solid grasp on what those goals and dreams actually are. Every product, no matter how mundane, needs to help its users reach for the stars—or at least make them feel that they are bettering themselves and improving their lifestyles. I never wanted to dust my living room furniture so much as I did when I first saw that Swiffer commercial. Did you?

The five steps described below will get you on your way. Remember: Think lifestyle and aspirations; don't get caught in the thinning middle; differentiate your brand, your message, and your products; and get out in the field and meet your customers—that's an essential part of the Five E's.

ACTION STEPS

STEP 1

Educate yourself on what it is you actually want to convey about the brand to your staff, your competitors, and the ultimate consumer. Make sure the focus of your business model is easily translated and ultimately communicated by everyone in your company. After all, if you and your key players don't have a cohesive message, how do you expect your company to have one? Find the right forum to communicate the direction, product value, and goals of the company. I always am surprised at finding out how many companies think they do this, but when I ask the executives in strategy sessions to identify the company's goals, I get as many different answers as there are executives in the room.

STEP 2

Explore the world your customers live in. Learn what their goals and dreams are, or at the very least come up with an idea of what you think they are. Don't concentrate only on what your company can produce; make it fit in with the customers' lives. Then determine what aspects of your product are most valuable to them. Is it price? Style? What is it they're looking for when buying your product, and does your brand message tap into those purchase influencers? There are several ways to determine your business's particular area of focus. Sometimes this effort requires an external focus, and it generally works best when it's based on unbiased opinions.

Don't be afraid to challenge your current business model. After all, the odds are that the method you used to develop and design the product or service you are offering was based on yesterday's customer's needs and marketed with yesterday's focus. Do you really think consumers are still making a decision about cable versus satellite that is based on the number of channels or the added services that come along with it? Today Direct TV is advertising that if you move, it will reinstall your satellite system for free. They are changing with the times, and so should you and your brand/product message.

Razors have elevated themselves to give users the optimum in comfort and performance. They help customers live larger with three or even four blades. How did consumers ever survive using just one blade? Even adding power to the razor, as in Gillette's Mach 3 Power, demonstrates the need to educate, not just sell. Gillette is trying to address the consumers' desire for the closest, most comfortable shave, and all this without nicks and tissues glued to their necks or legs.

STEP 3

Solidify that message and communicate it to the team, the retailer, and the consumer. Speak the correct language. American Eagle became the place that connected with teens. It stood for wearable fashion and connected with music and lifestyle to reflect the right image. It would have been easy not to challenge the leader in teen fashion, which arguably was Abercrombie & Fitch. But American Eagle viewed the teen market as its best opportunity to grow and, based on sales growth and store loyalty scores, ultimately replaced Abercrombie & Fitch as "the" place to shop. Abercrombie still maintains an aura of being the ultimate teen and young adult store, but as the priorities and spending habits of this group changed, so did the commitment to the store. American Eagle made sure to communicate its message internally, externally, and ultimately to the consumer through its product, its marketing approach, partnerships with charities, and the use of music. All those elements elevated and entertained, making the brand attractive to the teen consumer.

STEP 4

Segment your brand by lifestyle before user type and age. Don't get caught up in a one-dimensional focus. JC Penney converted private label brands into lifestyle brands, with Arizona Jeans and its Stafford brand standing for quality, value, and style. Many brands typically focus on one dimension of the target audience. As was stated earlier in this book, consumers today are more complex and diversified and allot a much shorter time to learning about a wider variety of needs and interests. JC Penney did a great job of not just selling private label jeans as many other retailers did. They weren't focused on simply selling more jeans than the national brands by lowering the price. They created Arizona Jeans as a lifestyle brand, not a one-dimensional product. Arizona Jeans really took off by personifying a particular lifestyle, one that was adventurous and vibrant, designed for the rugged outdoors. Jeans were only the beginning, and Arizona quickly migrated to other key categories, including fleece, and then went to outside apparel.

Building a brand involves connecting with consumers on a level that mirrors their lifestyle. Consumers have displayed over and over again that they are willing to spend more on products to which they personally relate. Market your brand toward lifestyle. It creates longevity, consumer connectivity, and word-of-mouth marketing. Nike doesn't just sell athletic shoes and apparel. It sells the whole experience of what most consumers strive for: excellence, commitment, expertise, skill, and the status of being the best.

STEP 5

Seek out opportunities that others don't. Jet Blue is a great example of this, finding a way to dominate its competitors in an industry that was in serious trouble. Jet Blue asked what customers wanted, and the answer was comfortable seats, entertainment, and on-time departures and arrivals. Then it asked what customers didn't want, and the answer was lousy food. The result: in-seat entertainment and the ability for customers to bring their own picnics.

Look for and embrace change and incorporate it regularly. The more you embed this philosophy into the culture of your organization, the better positioned you are to meet the changing needs of your customers and your business. Consumers are looking for change all the time; why shouldn't you? But don't change just for the sake of changing. Verify that the change is warranted and then proceed accordingly.

This is a balancing act that needs to be evaluated constantly, and when you see that your competitors have followed suit and the category is becoming saturated, change again. Be watchful for what I call "vacuum or bandwagon marketing"; that is what occurs when a business or category becomes so successful that it breeds competition. Find a product or brand that is doing well and see how many competitors jump into that space. When those bandwagon brands decide that they have had enough of a particular trend, they vacate it, opening up the category for the pure brands once again.

Take iPods, for instance. Every electronic company wanted to make MP3 players, and they are all doing that. Should Apple stop trying to market, upgrade, and sell iPods? Of course not, but think about how many more it will sell when the bandwagon brands decide to move on to the next trend and leave a vacuum in their wake. Think carefully before vacating a category of business. If that category plays to your core strengths and you can develop a following of core customers, ride it out.

THE FINAL WORD

Educate, Explore, Entertain, Elevate, and Evaluate your way to growing your business. Take the time to structure a strategic day with your team's key players, utilize the research that is available beyond your own sales data, and learn what the customers aspire to, what they think of your brand or service, why they buy it, and why they don't. And then evaluate, test, and evaluate again—you just might discover a whole new opportunity to maximize your strengths and eradicate your weaknesses.

Make your customer a partner in designing and defining your brand.

Index